Shortcut Cooking

Shortcut Cooking

A Guide to Preparing Quick but Delectable Meals

Charlotte Erickson

Contemporary Books, Inc.
Chicago

Library of Congress Cataloging in Publication Data

Erickson, Charlotte Helen Zimmer

   Shortcut cooking.

   Includes index.
   1. Cookery.   2. Home economics.   I. Title.
TX652.E64   1981   641.5′55   80-70645
ISBN 0-8092-5887-0 pbk.

Prior to revision, this book was originally published
as *The Working Person's Cookbook* by Chilton Book Company

Copyright © 1981, 1979 by Charlotte Erickson
All rights reserved
Published by Contemporary Books, Inc.
180 North Michigan Avenue, Chicago, Illinois 60601
Manufactured in the United States of America
Library of Congress Catalog Card Number: 80-70645
International Standard Book Number: 0-8092-5887-0

Published simultaneously in Canada by
Beaverbooks, Ltd.
150 Lesmill Road
Don Mills, Ontario M3B 2T5
Canada

TO BUSY PEOPLE EVERYWHERE

*My thanks and gratitude to all those wonderful busy
and working people who so freely contributed
their time-saving ideas, their shortcuts,
and their many time saving recipes.*

MICROWAVE OVEN
This symbol indicates that the recipe can be adapted to your microwave oven. It appears alongside the instructions at the point in the recipe where it would be used. Oven units vary, so refer to manufacturer's instructions.

FOOD PROCESSOR
When you see this symbol alongside ingredients or instructions in a recipe, your food processor can be used to grate, shred, chop, grind, or perform other time-consuming operations.

SLOW COOKER
This symbol indicates that a recipe is easily adapted to a slow cooker. For specifics, see manufacturer's instructions for your model.

PANTRY GOODS
Recipes which can be assembled at a moment's notice from ingredients frequently found in your pantry or freezer.

CLOCK
This symbol appears on recipes that are great to fix ahead and serve later. Some recipes have ingredients that require marinating or refrigeration for several hours; others are simply easy to have on hand, ready to pop into the oven direct from your freezer.

TIMER
Look for this symbol when you need a recipe that can be prepared in 20 minutes or less.

Contents

Preface

This book has been specifically written for the working person. There's a growing trend toward spending less time in the kitchen and sharing household tasks, including cooking. Often husband and wife work, even when there are small children. People also are more involved in community activities, as well as sports and hobbies, leaving less time for K.P. duty. Since time at home is usually limited, most people prefer to replace kitchen toil with more pleasurable pursuits. *Shortcut Cooking* will help you prepare delicious, nutritious meals while spending less time in the kitchen.

This book is also chock-full of money-saving and time-saving ideas that have been shared with me by countless working people. I bet you have wondered how the Joneses down the street manage their household chores and still stay involved in all their activities. Are you always running behind schedule, wishing you had an extra pair of hands? Are you always resolving that things are going to be different next week? Perhaps *Shortcut Cooking* can help you organize your time better, leaving you more relaxed with more leisure time for yourself. Along with ideas on good nutrition and suggestions for quickie meals that everyone likes and anyone can prepare, this book also includes a chapter filled with helpful hints, including how to cope with morning bedlam—or getting out of the house in 30 minutes flat.

We all know that there are a multitude of prepared foods sold at the supermarkets today; meals can come from freezer to oven (or microwave) to table with no effort at all. Nearby fast-food chains and carryout restaurants or delicatessens also have a variety of foods that can be picked up and brought home, again with no effort on the part of the homemaker. But there are drawbacks to a continual diet of fast and prepared foods. Not only do they become monotonous and terribly expensive, but also many of them just aren't as palate pleasing or as nutritious as good food should be. Preparing or supervising the preparation of three square meals a day every day can be an intimidating task. *Shortcut Cooking* can show you how these chores can be done with ease, usually saving a lot of time.

There are many canned, frozen, and dried products that represent an enormous savings when the time involved in peeling, chopping, or initial cooking steps is considered. Whenever possible these time-saving ingredients are used throughout the book. However, don't expect to find ten different ways to use Hamburger Helper.

All the recipes in this book have been thoroughly tested; they are simple to make, with easy-to-follow instructions. The novice and even children will have marvelous results with the recipes. Included are quick and easy gourmet recipes for those "special" occasions, such as birthdays, anniversaries, and the arrival of out-of-town guests. See how candles and wine can turn a "leftover meal" into a festive repast.

ACKNOWLEDGMENTS

My special thanks to Hildy Iverson, who worked untiringly typing the manuscript, testing recipes and evaluating the food processors and other appliances.

Thanks to all the manufacturers who sent us their appliances to be tested and evaluated: American Electric Corp., G. S. Blakeslee and Co., Bon Jour Imports Corp., Braun North America, Farberware-Kidde, Hamilton Beach Division of Scovill Manufacturing, Hobart Corp., McGraw-Edison Co., Moulinex Products, Omnichef Corp., Oster Corp., Sunbeam Appliance Co., Vita Mix Corp. and Waring Products Division.

For information used in preparing this book, I am grateful to The University of Illinois School of Agriculture, The United States Department of Agriculture, and The University of Illinois Homemakers Service.

Shortcut Cooking

Introduction

SHORTCUTS AND OTHER TIME SAVING IDEAS

Our local and sometimes even our national news services carry stories about superachievers. Sammy Superachiever works at three jobs, attends night school, jogs ten miles every day, and is running for political office. Sylvia Superachiever, the mother of seven children, efficiently combines two careers and is now heading the local charity drive, as well as writing a dissertation for her PhD. These people come in many shapes, sizes, and varieties, but they all have some of the following things in common. Although she is never mentioned in the newspapers, usually lurking in the background is a marvelous saint of a nonworking wife or mother in the case of Sammy Superachiever, or a housekeeper or mother, aunt, or other relative in the case of Sylvia Superachiever. Often a combination of several people can be found after sufficient probing. Usually these superstars enjoy little or no family life —only when the cameraman and reporters are around.

Rule 1: Don't compare yourself unfavorably with these superachievers. They are in a class by themselves. Just accept that an in-depth probe will reveal much more than the well-polished exterior exposed to the public.

Rule 2: Accept the fact that the lack of time will restrict your ability to do all the things you would like to do. Don't set your goals too high. This is particularly true if you have children living at home.

A Little Organization Helps

Make a list of weekly chores or jobs you really consider important, then another list of things you would like to do but could get along without. These items should be listed in order of their importance, e.g., doing the laundry would precede removing fingerprints from the hall wall.

Next make a list of the weekly tasks that could be handled by some other member of the family or hired or borrowed help. How many times have you heard someone remark, "Whenever I do thus and such it's never right anyway"? The point is to encourage more work around the house on the part of *Others*. Be sure that the person understands completely what he is to do, when, and how. Be very specific, especially if it is a first-time experience. Don't expect perfection, at least not in the beginning. Be cheerful and be complimentary (only give sincere compliments) when chores are finished, no matter how poorly a job was executed. Find something positive to say even if it's only, "Well how nice, you've finished!" Then gently tell the person how to improve next time. There's always the possibility that a person will deliberately try to botch every job with the express purpose of not being asked again. More on this later.

As you review your list ask yourself, "Is there any particular reason why I have to do the weekly grocery shopping? Why can't so-and-so make a weekly (or biweekly) trip to the cleaners?"

It is not uncommon to feel a loss of importance when you finish going over your list and see that there really are few things someone else couldn't assist you with or do entirely. This is not to suggest that you should spend all your free time sitting around eating chocolates and bonbons and watching soap operas while everyone else is working. Simply try to get your housework into the proper perspective and allow sufficient leisure time to do the fun things in life. You don't want to become a drudge.

HOW TO LIGHTEN YOUR WORK LOAD

Hiring Outside Help

If you are *working full time* or have a heavy load of activities and responsibilities, try to hire some household help. High school and college students are often eager to obtain this sort of work. They are a particularly good source of help in areas where steady weekly help is difficult to find, and they're usually less expensive than professional domestic help. You'll be amazed at what a difference having help for just four hours on Saturday morning can make. Consider the matter seriously!

Cooking More Than One Meal at a Time

In order to spend a minimum amount of time in the kitchen, the busy person must utilize time to its fullest. This can be done in several ways. If you are cooking something on the stove that needs a watchful eye but not too much effort on your part, you can start preparing tomorrow's meal at the same time. This may sound terribly involved, but it really isn't. For example, you are fixing chop suey for dinner, your chop suey is simmering for a half-hour, and your rice is also cooking. Why not brown your meat for the next night's stew, add vegetables, cover, and let it simmer all evening, developing that rich flavor that comes from long, slow cooking? Refrigerate just before bedtime and all you'll have to do the next night is warm it up.

To be truly efficient, you should be making enough stew for two nights, freezing half of it for a future meal, and serving the other half the following evening. That way you would have done three or four nights' cooking in one evening.

A freezer is the busy person's best friend. If you don't have one, put it on the top of your list of things to save for. See page 24.

Organizing Your Kitchen

Having your kitchen efficiently organized makes cooking not only more enjoyable but also less time- and energy-consuming. From now on be conscious of time-wasting occurrences, such as not being able to find something or not having a piece of equipment or an ingredient that's needed. You might also evaluate some habits that might need changing; we all have acquired some bad habits. Maybe it's just a small thing, like not cleaning up after yourself as you go along. I'm quite familiar with that bad habit; instead of rinsing and putting all the dirty dishes in the dishwasher as you go along, it is easier to dump them all in the sink, right? Wrong. In the long run you waste more time because you can't get at your sink properly (dishes are in your way), and your counter space gets cluttered, not leaving you any room to work. If you don't have a dishwasher, have some hot suds ready and soak or wash and rinse out your dishes as you go along. Let them air dry on a dish rack.

PLACEMENT OF KITCHEN EQUIPMENT. Food preparation will go more smoothly if your kitchen is well stocked with the ingredients you use most frequently. Where you store them is also of prime importance. A good way to visualize your kitchen is to divide it up into different areas, such as preparation, cooking, serving, clean up (this includes your kitchen sink area), and storage areas. Then put all the items related to these chores in their appropriate places. If drawer space is at a premium or inconveniently located, keep cooking utensils (spatulas, wooden stirring spoons, wire whisks, etc.) adjacent to your stove in a decorative crock, pitcher, or even a stone planter. Keeping your spices and condiments near the stove (but away from direct heat) is just good common sense. You don't need to be an Einstein to understand that keeping your coffee in a cupboard above the counter where your coffee maker is kept is going to save you time and steps. Use a dry measuring cup for coffee instead of a spoon, e.g., if you normally use 4 tablespoons of coffee when making a pot, use a ¼ measuring cup. Keep it in your coffee can. This won't save a lot of time, but every little bit helps. Many steps, time, and motion can be saved by thinking through your entire kitchen and where you store things in relation to where they're used.

All baking supplies should be kept in one general area, adjacent to your electric mixer. These include such things as flour, sugar, vanilla and other extracts, baking soda, baking powder, and measuring cups. Store frequently used items where you can reach them easily. In high or less accessible storage areas place equipment and supplies that are seldom used, such as punch bowls and cups that are used exclusively for entertaining large groups, or special gelatin molds with seasonal design that may only be used once or twice a year. In a small or crowded kitchen this may not be possible, but try to keep from overcrowding your cupboards. You're wasting minutes each time you have to shove and search around for some lost item.

Dishes, silverware, and serving pieces should be stored somewhere between the dishwasher (or sink) and the table for very obvious reasons. The smaller the triangle between these three points, the better. The exception is when you have a portable dishwasher that can be moved readily. In this case, the dishes and silverware should be stored as close to the table as possible, rather than near the sink.

Use drawer dividers for cutlery and silverware. Keep knives sharp; cutting bread, cakes, meats, and vegetables goes much faster when knives are sharp. A magnetic knife holder mounted inside a cabinet door is a good out-of-the-way, yet convenient, place to store your knives when space is limited. Knives kept in a drawer with other utensils will dull much faster. Have a portable cutting board that you can use at your sink when preparing vegetables, as well as in other areas of the kitchen. Be sure you have a vegetable peeler for quick, easy peeling. (They are now available for both left- and right-handed people.) Magnetic potholders that cling to the side or front of the stove are most convenient. Your potholders will always be where you need them.

Increasing Your Counter Space and Storage Area

When either storage space or counter space is in short supply, there are a number of things you can do. First, check all your cabinets and cupboards to make sure that available space isn't being used by equipment, serving pieces, or accessories that haven't been used since you received them as wedding gifts. Anything that hasn't been used in the past year should be either stored elsewhere or packed away (unless you can bring yourself to discarding or giving it away).

A small strip of pegboard can turn a plain wall area into an attractive, convenient, and much used storage area. Chopping blocks on wheels with storage area underneath are also a wonderful thing to have. These come in various sizes and shapes and can be found at your building supply or kitchen cabinet showrooms and centers, as well as specialty kitchen stores. Some are completely enclosed or have drawer or cupboard space; others are open all the way around. Less expensive are the metal utility carts on wheels. Kitchen appliances such as mixers, toaster ovens, and coffee makers can be used right in place on the utility cart, allowing you more work space on your kitchen counters. Instead of a butcher-block top you might want a ceramic top that is great to set hot things on for cooling. This cart can be rolled to your table and also be used as a serving cart.

A fold-down shelf can also supply extra work area. This can be made of wood, ceramic tile, or laminated plastic. Check the housewares section in your local department or variety store, or hardware store the next time you go. There are many accessories available that extend storage space, such as stacking units, turntables, one- or two-tier cup hangers, and special racks that attach inside cabinet doors that hold spices, lids of pots and pans, paper towel and waxed paper holders, etc.

An uncluttered counter top is desirable; however, if space is limited this may not be possible. With a critical eye, appraise all the items stored on your counter top. Do you really need all those canisters there? Perhaps the cookie jar could be kept in the eating or dining area, and maybe the toaster too. An uncluttered counter top is also much easier to clean. Frequently used electrical appliances are best kept out for easy accessibility. Often they are too cumbersome to move, and if not kept in a convenient location, they're not likely to get much use.

If your home has more than one level, have baskets at the top and bottom of the stairs. Anything that needs to be taken down or up can be put into these baskets. Make it a cardinal rule that whoever traverses the stairs take the basket with them and empty it. Have the baskets color coordinated, a different one for the top and the bottom. That way you'll know where the basket belongs and won't have two at the top and none at the bottom.

Using Timers Effectively

Minute timers, such as those in your kitchen or on your stove, are great for reminding you about things beside cooking—when your clothes in the dryer will be done, for example. (Taking them out as soon as they are dry will eliminate most of your ironing.) Use small traveling alarm clocks to remind you of important chores when you are outside or in other areas of the house. A phone call or interruption can easily distract you; these portable timers will keep you on "schedule."

Lists, Lists, Lists

Keep a steno pad or some other small convenient booklet handy. Each page can be a separate list which, when taken care, is just torn out and thrown away. One list, for example, can be things that you need the next time you go to the local shopping center. Another list could be things you want to accomplish during the following week or over the weekend. Make lists of things you'd like other people in your family to do and let each member pick one or two projects on the list. If you post these lists on a bulletin board in the kitchen or hallway, each person can initial the chores he has selected for himself and cross them off as they are completed. A reward for the person finishing first is a good incentive. Make lists of things you wish to buy, such as gifts for birthdays, anniversaries, and weddings, rather than making a last minute dash before the appointed hour. Write ideas for your gifts on the list and keep an eye open each time you go shopping. Also keep these ideas in mind when reading the local newspaper.

SALES. Take advantage of special sales, and order items over the phone whenever possible. Many stores now have a service charge for delivery, but they are usually very small indeed. You can save the price in gas (driving there and back), plus the time you have "wasted." Remember, your time is worth money too.

ENTERTAINING. If you are entertaining or having house guests, have a list for that occasion also. Prepare a menu and list all ingredients you need to purchase. Include flowers, candles, liquor and mixes. You may also want to list what you're going to wear, which accessories you are going to use, and so forth. Then in the midst of the excitement you will not have to tax your brain trying to remember all these things. It also makes it easier for someone else to assist you if you have it all written down. (Incidentally, if you are a commuter, the time spent going to and from work provides a marvelous opportunity to make up these lists.)

VACATIONS. Keep a list of what you'd like to pack before vacations. If you're a camping family, have one list for just your camping supplies. Take the list along and add to it (during your trip) all the things you forgot or additional items that would be nice to have along. Now when you return home, you'll have a complete list for next time. Do the same with your clothing and personal care items. Have different lists for summer and winter trips if these are in your plans, as well as week-long and weekend trips. If you save these old lists, you can pack in a wink next time. Have a separate list for your children, which includes such things as wallets, money, sunglasses, hats, games, cameras, and film. Each family member (who can read) should be responsible for his or her own packing. We duplicate our packing list; one is always kept on file. The other is used when packing and each item is crossed off as it is packed. When making additions and deletions, be sure to keep file copy current.

> Here lies a poor woman, who always was tired;
> She lived in a house where help was not hired.
> Her last words on earth were: "Dear friends, I am going
> Where washing ain't done, nor sweeping, nor sewing;
> But everything there is exact to my wishes;
> For where they don't eat, there's no washing of dishes."
> AUTHOR UNKNOWN

We all probably feel like the poor woman in the poem at one time or another. However, let's not wait as long as she did for a little rest and relaxation. Try to organize your household duties in such a way that you'll have time for the fun things in life.

MAKE IT EASY FOR OTHERS TO HELP

Whether you are living alone, with just an occasional guest, or have a multimember household, the following ideas should be of considerable help in aiding others to help you. Margaret Sanik of Cornell University, in her study "Time And Household Productivity," found that women still spend considerably more time doing household chores than men or other members of the family. Mrs. Sanik said that even in families that claim their households are run on a 50-50 basis, she found these proportions were "way off." According to her studies, employed childless wives spend 3.7 hours per day to their husbands' 1.2 hours per day on tasks around the house. Employed wives with one child spend 5.1 hours per day around their house to their husbands' 1.9 hours per day. Perhaps we could equalize these numbers more by making it easier for others to help, or by at least making it more difficult for them not to help you. The following ideas should be helpful.

Make it easy for others to help—that should be your motto always. If someone has lived with you in the same house for a number of years and still can't empty the dishwasher because he or she "doesn't know where anything belongs," label everything. As long as everyone in the family can read, everything should be put in its proper place without any further ado.

Labels

There are little labeling machines that can be purchased in variety and stationery stores. They have plastic tapes in various sizes and colors. I use these since the labels look so neat and are so easy to apply and remove when changes are in order. They also wipe clean with a sponge when necessary. Choose colors that blend in; you don't want the tapes to be a focal point. For those of you in the over-40 crowd, choose the widest tape with the largest lettering available, so that reading is possible without putting on those specs. Put self-sticking labels on the edges of all your cupboards or pantry shelves, indicating where wine glasses, milk glasses, juice glasses, dinner plates, canned foods, pots and pans—all items are stored.

PANTRY. However you arrange your pantry or cupboard shelves, if you have fruit cans and juices in one area, label them and then anyone can put the groceries away in such a manner that you can find everything. Just recently I observed a refrigerator that was labeled (on the inside, of course). Shelves were labeled leftovers, condiments, salad greens, miscellaneous vegetables, etc. Even the refrigerator door shelves were labeled, as well as the shelves in the freezer compartment.

LINEN CLOSETS. Linen closets are another place where labels—*twin sheet tops, twin sheet bottoms, queen size tops, queen size bottoms, pillows, guest towels, bath towels*—help enormously. You'll be amazed at what a help this is even for yourself. Closets and cupboards tend to stay straightened up much longer with this labeling system. Anyone who wishes to change sheets on a bed or who is looking for supplies doesn't have to poke around and mess up your closets.

MEDICINE CABINET. The medicine cabinet is another place where labeling pays off. Not only does it help keep your cabinet in order, but also it makes it much easier for others, including baby-sitters or guests, to find what they are looking for. Use such labels as *first aid, cough and cold medicine,* and *prescriptions.* Keep all your Band-Aids, gauze pads, and adhesive tape with your first aid sign. The cough and cold medicines would include decongestants and cough syrups. Not only will this help you find what you're looking for, but also it will help whoever cleans these shelves from time to time to know where everything should be placed.

How often have you had someone clean or straighten out a closet, cupboard, or drawer only to find that you can't find anything after it has been "cleaned." This manner of labeling will eliminate all that. Remember, try to label as much of your storage space as possible. Where it's impractical to label the shelves, perhaps labels could be put on cabinet doors.

PLANTS. Do your plants sometimes suffer neglect because you don't have time to water or fertilize them? Measure the amount of water you normally give your plant. Make a label with these instructions on them, as well as whether the plant's to be watered weekly or biweekly. (Any plant requiring more than biweekly care should do you a favor and expire. You don't have time for it.) For example, your label would read "¾ cup—weekly." Not only will you be able to delegate emergency care, but also your neighbor who plant-sits when you're on vacation will be grateful.

Notes and Instructions

Leaving notes and directions around the house also helps. One family I know has complete instructions for using the washer and dryer, typed neatly and encased in plastic and hung over the machines for all to read. Everyone has his or her own way of doing these chores, and it would take only a few minutes to write them down in a concise, neat manner. Stationery stores have plastic sheets to encase these instructions; most supermarkets have machines that laminate anything in plastic. This makes the instructions more durable, easy to wipe off, and eliminates the necessity of recopying them from time to time. When Johnny says he needs a clean gym suit for class tomorrow morning, just send him on his merry little way to the laundry room. You will be amazed at how self-sufficient everyone can become and how much of your time will be saved. Accept any offers you might receive to help you get organized—don't let your pride interfere.

Management Efficiency in the Home

An interesting story recently appeared in the Chicago newspapers telling of a Dr. John M. Samuels, Assistant Professor of Industrial Engineering at Penn State University. Apparently, and not unlike other husbands, he had been telling his wife that she was a poor organizer and not efficient (sound familiar?) He tells this story. "One Saturday morning my wife got me out of bed and said, 'Okay, wiseguy, you're going to organize our kitchen more efficiently.'" He continued, "Well, a guy's gotta have a sense of humor about the whole thing," so he got to work. The first thing that he did was to take everything out of the cabinets. Then they analyzed all the chores, down to even the smallest details like how to make a cup of coffee. He applied all the ideas of management efficiency to organizing the kitchen. "The whole idea is to make work easier to do and in less time. If you have to work, it may as well be done efficiently," said Dr. Samuels, who at one time was Production Engineer for General Motors. A stool was placed at the kitchen counter so the work could be done in a sitting position. Said Dr. Samuels, ''one of the golden rules of industry is that people should have a place to sit or be comfortable where they're working. It's amazing how many kitchens don't have stools.'' So the next time your husband, mother-in-law, son, or daughter suggests that you get organized, ask him or her to do it for you or help you do it. Not a bad idea!

The Persistent Botcher

If you feel that someone near and dear to you is deliberately botching up every or most tasks with the express purpose of not being asked to do them, again don't make accusations, which would only lead to denials anyway. First, ask which task appeals to him or her most. If that doesn't work, assign the person very simple and menial tasks, such as taking out the garbage, tying up newspapers and taking them to the recycling depository, and running errands. If he or she forgets things while on an errand, it will be necessary to go back. The idea is not to give up on this sort of an individual. Everybody should carry his or her own weight.

SHOPPING TIPS

Remember that time is your most precious commodity. Don't fritter it away on useless things. Except in very unusual cases, grocery shopping should be confined to once a week. Try to do your shopping in ''off hours'' when the aisles are empty and the clerks have time to assist you. If at all possible, stay away from the stores on Saturday mornings.

The Shopping List

Make a list. Keep a pad and pencil handy in your kitchen and add ingredients as you use them up. We keep ours attached with a magnetic clip to our refrigerator door. Under threat of five years at hard labor, everybody adds any ingredients that they use up or finish, or any that are almost used up. This includes nonfood items too, such as lunch bags, toothpaste, and cleanser.

When you finish a bag of noodles, assuming that this is an item that you would normally use, immediately jot down ''noodles'' on your shopping list for that week. When you use a can of soup or a package of frozen vegetables, again put it on the list. This way you will always have a very well stocked kitchen, making last minute cooking much easier and saving many trips to the store or to your next-door neighbor. Have all the ingredients for a few favorite family quickie recipes on hand at all times. Also, have things, that can be whipped up with little or no effort on hand in case unexpected company drops by (see page 57). With this method your list will always be up to date and you won't have to sit down and make up a complete new list before going to the store. You may also want to make a list of the food that you intend to prepare the following week and add any additional ingredients that may be required.

Menu Plans

Make a list of menu plans for the week (this can be as simple as just listing an entrée for each day). Make a notation after each entry as follows.

Sunday—Pot roast, potatoes, carrots, and onions
Monday—Spaghetti (sauce in freezer), tossed salad
Tuesday—Corned beef and cabbage (see recipe page 63); put all
     ingredients into slow cooker in morning before leaving
Wednesday—Leftovers
Thursday—Reuben sandwiches with leftover corned beef
Friday—Meatloaf, baked potatoes, coleslaw (see recipe page 134)
Saturday—Invited for dinner at the Bauers

When writing up menus always list the dishes that require the longest cooking first, and the shortest last. This way, whoever is preparing dinner can just work through your list and not worry about timing. This is especially important for the novice.

Posting this list in your kitchen will eliminate serious early morning thinking or planning when you're really not into first gear. Any instructions that need to be done early in the day, such as "remove meat from freezer" or "put meat in slow cooker" should be included. This is especially important for people who don't really "wake up" until later in the day. Also, it will allow whoever gets home first to start dinner! That's why a more complete list with instructions for cooking could be a very big help. Avoid foods that require a lot of last minute attention or that won't "hold up" beyond a certain serving time; keep these menus as reference for future meals. You may have several menus that really work well for you; if so, make copies and use them over from time to time. Have a recipe box where favorites are written on cards for handy reference. Include complete instructions, so anyone can follow the recipe.

"Specials"

A money-saving idea is to shop "specials." Check the newspapers and see which meat is on sale that particular week. Remember, though, a cut of meat is not a bargain if your family doesn't like it and won't eat it. Because meat is probably the single most expensive item on your grocery list, a little thought in buying this commodity pays big rewards. Shopping at the same store each week saves time. The shopper will quickly get to know where everything is displayed, and precious time looking for various items will be saved. Wise consumers know that the highest priced items at the grocery store are usually those at eye level. It's the smart shopper who looks above and below. Research also shows that once a shopper picks up an item, it's quite likely to end up in the grocery cart.

Cultivate the friendship of your local butcher. He can save you a lot of time and money. Be thoughtful; don't arrive at the store ten minutes before closing time and ask him to bone and skin a half-dozen chicken breasts. Rather, call him early in the day with your order, so he can have it ready when you stop by just before closing. Even very large supermarkets will be happy to do this for you. Select a butcher who has good quality meat, and don't shop on price alone. Many stores make a practice of selling meat at a cheaper price, but their meat cuts have a great deal more fat and bone. This will save you nothing, and may even cost you more in the long run. If you have the freezer space, buy meat which is on sale in large quantities (providing these are cuts that you would normally use) and put them in your freezer.

Shopping Alone

Another time and money-saver is shopping alone. Children pestering you to buy this and that is costly as well as time-consuming. Always shop after you have eaten if you're trying to save money; avoid impulse buying and stick to your list.

Having a complete list ready at all times will also enable others to shop for you (the biggest time-saver of all). Don't expect perfection the first time; try not to complain about all the things brought home which were not on your list. This usually only happens the first few times; it soon wears off.

Frozen Foods

When checking out at the grocery store, either ask the bagger to pack your frozen food in separate bags or boxes, or do so yourself. This is particularly helpful if your freezer is not located in the kitchen.

Just take your bag or box to the freezer and unload it directly, thereby saving the time and effort of double handling.

Meat that is not to be frozen should be stored in the coldest part of your refrigerator. Store canned foods in a cool, dry place. Shelves over the stove or on top of the refrigerator (where heat from the refrigerator is trapped) are not ideal locations for canned goods.

Pantry Goods

If you have sufficient room for a sizable inventory of staples and canned goods, you may wish to date everything at the time of purchase. Use felt markers and put the month and year on top of the can or on the label, e.g., 2/81. That way you can always use the can with the oldest date first. Try to rotate everything, so that it is used within a year, as flavor and nutrition can deteriorate somewhat after one year's storage time. (Canned goods can keep indefinitely as long as the cans are not rusted, leaking, or "ballooned.") Because of rapid inflation the price on each item will usually tell which one is the oldest, as that date will have the lowest price. However, you still don't know exactly how old it is. Some canned and packaged goods now also have freshness dates on their labels, but they are often difficult to find and are often in code. Marking them with a felt marker gives you this information at a glance.

Spices and Herbs

Spices and herbs lose their strength and flavor with age, so it is good to buy them in small quantities only. They should be stored in a cool, dry place away from direct sunlight. You can tell if your herbs are still good by rubbing some between the palms of your hands and then smelling them; if there is a strong aroma, the herbs are good, and if there is no aroma, replace them with a fresh supply. For whole spices (whole cloves, cardamon seeds) use a mortar and pestle. If you don't have that, hammer them on a wooden block and use the same test.

HELPFUL HINTS FOR THE SINGLE OR TWO-PERSON HOUSEHOLD

For the single or two-person household with just a small freezer compartment above the refrigerator, a seal-and-heat unit would be very practical. Seal-and-heat bags lend themselves especially well to individual or small portions, and they take up a minimum amount of space in your small freezer. Be sure to label and date each package clearly; spaghetti sauce and chili look very much alike when frozen in a pouch!

Even though they are larger, the 20-ounce packages of frozen vegetables are best for the small household. You can shake out the exact amount you need, seal the bag, and return it to the freezer. This is not as easily done with the smaller packages. Fish and seafood may also be purchased in large or small bags where they are individually frozen. These are preferable to the packages that come frozen in a solid piece.

You'll find the following table an invaluable help in dividing recipes. (*Note:* a "pinch" is as much as can be taken between tip of finger and thumb.)

DIVIDED-RECIPE EQUIVALENTS

½ of ¼ teaspoon = ⅛ teaspoon or 2 pinches
½ of 1 tablespoon = 1½ teaspoons
½ of ¼ cup = 2 tablespoons
½ of ⅓ cup = 2⅔ tablespoons (approximately 3 tablespoons)
½ of ½ cup = ¼ cup
½ of ⅔ cup = ⅓ cup
½ of ¾ cup = ¼ cup plus 2 tablespoons (approximately ⅓ cup)
½ of 1 cup = ½ cup
½ of 1 liquid ounce = 1 tablespoon
½ of ½ pint = ½ cup
½ of 1 pint = 1 cup
½ of 1 quart = 2 cups
½ of 1 gallon = 2 quarts

⅓ of ¼ teaspoon = a pinch
⅓ of ½ teaspoon = 2 pinches
⅓ of 1 tablespoon = 1 teaspoon
⅓ of 2 tablespoons = 2 teaspoons
⅓ of ¼ cup = 1 tablespoon plus 1 teaspoon
⅓ of ⅓ cup = 1¾ tablespoons (approximately 2 tablespoons)
⅓ of ½ cup = 2⅔ tablespoons (approximately 3 tablespoons)
⅓ of ⅔ cup = 3½ tablespoons
⅓ of ¾ cup = 4 tablespoons
⅓ of 1 cup = ⅓ cup
⅓ of 1 liquid ounce = 2 teaspoons
⅓ of ½ pint = ⅓ cup
⅓ of 1 pint = ⅔ cup
⅓ of 1 quart = 1⅓ cup
⅓ of 1 gallon = 1⅓ quarts or 5⅓ cups

Remember that when you are dividing recipes, it's usually okay to round off your measurements, i.e., when a recipe you are dividing in half asks for ¾ cup milk, use ⅓ cup instead of the more accurate ¼ cup plus 2 tablespoons. Just remember that our grandmothers probably didn't even have measuring cups! Recipes are only a guide.

KEEPING THE KITCHEN CLEAN

Kitchens, much like bathrooms, seem to get that "lived-in look" all too soon. Keeping the kitchen shipshape means simply keeping at it. Wipe the top of the sink, range, and counters every day. Keep a cellulose sponge handy for quick clean-ups. Spills on the floor should be wiped up immediately. Once dry, they will be harder to remove and may leave a permanent stain.

Remove clutter from cabinets and drawers. The next time you clean your kitchen cabinets, try to discard as much as possible. Pack away any kitchen equipment not used within the past year, as well as anything you have duplicates of and really don't need. (See Getting Rid of Clutter, page 19). An uncluttered kitchen (this includes cabinets and drawers, as well as counter tops) is much easier to keep clean and orderly.

For daily cleaning I like a liquid cleaner that I keep in a spray bottle. It cleans chrome, stainless steel, Formica (laminated plastic), the baked enamel on stoves, refrigerators, dishwashers, woodwork, and walls very easily without any smudge or smear marks. It also cuts into grease and hard dirt with just a wipe of a damp towel or sponge. Cleaning compounds are a matter of preference; try several and see which ones you like the best. Try to give the kitchen a daily once-over lightly.

There is a correct and an incorrect way of doing many things. Often you can save time by avoiding a mess in the first place. For example, when you pour coffee into your coffee maker, or fill sugar bowls, canisters, and salt and pepper shakers, do it over the sink. If salt and pepper shakers have small openings, use a funnel. (This goes for other narrow-necked containers as well.) This will save lots of time in counter and floor clean-ups. The same thing should be done when you pour food from one container into another, such as from a pan to a serving container. When making bread or cookie crumbs with an automatic food grinder, attach a large plastic bag with a rubberband to the grinder outlet. Presto, no crumbs on the floor or counter. These are just a few of the ways you can avoid messy clean-ups; you'll find dozens of others when you start thinking about it.

Use oven-to-table cookware whenever possible, as this eliminates a lot of clean-up work. Serve a whole meal on a platter whenever applicable, e.g., a roast in the center of a large platter surrounded by baked potatoes and steamed carrot sticks with parsley butter. Not only is this an attractive way of serving, but also it makes for less passing around at the dinner table, as well as fewer dishes.

If your eating area is a long distance from your cooking area, use trays or a serving cart to transport food and dishes, as well as to clean up after meals. Cover seldom used dishes, cups, glassware, and serving pieces with plastic. You can use clear plastic that comes in a roll or the very large plastic baggies, as well as some vinyl covers that are made especially for this purpose. These covers are usually available in the larger department stores, as well as some mail order catalogues.

Cleaning Kitchen Cabinets and Drawers

One of the more necessary items in a kitchen is a phone conveniently placed with an extra long cord that can reach to every corner of the kitchen. Not only will this allow you to cancel Johnny's guitar lesson and make an appointment with the pediatrician while preparing dinner, but also it will allow you to tidy up your kitchen while chatting with a dear friend who is in the hospital.

A very common complaint of people who work is that they miss or are unable to keep up their social contacts because "they don't have time." There is absolutely no reason why you can't straighten out the silverware drawer while chatting with your ex-roommate. A phone shoulder rest will allow you to use both hands for various jobs while conversing on the phone. These tidying up jobs in the kitchen do not take a lot of concentration. It is easy to combine them with pleasant conversation. It is amazing how much more pleasurable it is tidying up your kitchen, your cupboards, your counter, and your drawers if you "reward" yourself with a long chat with someone you would not have had time to call otherwise.

The converse of this is also true. When you receive a call from someone you haven't heard from in a long time and you don't want to cut them off, just make yourself a little sudsy water and start cleaning wherever you think needs it most. You just might end up having the cleanest kitchen in town (and the most fun doing it).

Another idea is to keep a mending basket nearby. Use your telephone time to sew on buttons or hem a skirt. Pressing and ironing is another job that doesn't take much concentration or moving around, which can easily be done while using the telephone.

Cleaning Your Refrigerator

The best time to clean your refrigerator is just before you go grocery shopping when it is most empty. If it is tidied up each week just before shopping time, a major cleaning can be postponed for several weeks. It also allows you to take a quick inventory of what's needed before shopping. Here again, clean spills immediately; fresh spills usually wipe up with just a swipe. Once they have dried, however, it can be a major job. When major cleaning of the refrigerator is in order, remove food from one shelf at a time, working from top to bottom, and keep the items in separate places. You will be able to return food to the refrigerator very quickly this way. Use baking soda to wipe down the inside of the refrigerator. *Never use scouring or cleansing powder* on the inside of a refrigerator or freezer; it will damage the finish.

Cleaning and Defrosting Your Freezer

Small freezer units that are not frost-free and are a part of your refrigerator can be defrosted quickly with the use of a hand-held hair dryer. Unplug refrigerator. Turn the blow dryer on as hot as it will go, and the ice will loosen quickly. Don't let ice build up more than ½ inch on your refrigerator or freezer. Excessive ice build-up acts as insulation. If you notice excessive ice build-up, check your gasket for air leakage; it may need to be replaced. Keeping your refrigerator door closed as much as possible and your food covered will also cut down on frost build-up in your freezer or refrigerator, so when you start to prepare dinner, remove all the ingredients you will need at one time.

An ingenious husband devised the most remarkable way of defrosting and cleaning a freezer that is stored in the garage or basement near a drain. Remove all the food. Connect a garden hose to a hot water tap and attach an adjustable nozzle to other end. Hose your freezer down with warm water; it will defrost almost instantly. The water will run down the drain or out of the garage, and your freezer will be defrosted and sparkling clean in 10 to 15 minutes. This method can be used on upright freezers and on chest-type freezers that have a drain in the bottom.

Winter is a marvelous time for defrosting your freezer, since in most parts of the country you can put your food in cardboard cartons and set them outside as you are defrosting. If you live in a warm climate or are defrosting in the summer time, pack all your frozen foods in cartons and cover them with newspapers or blankets or put them in a thermal chest if one is available. Defrost when you have little or no ice cream or sherbet. *Never* use an ice pick or knife to pry ice loose; you might puncture the refrigerator tubing or coils, which could let poisonous ammonia gases escape. Plastic ice scrapers used to scrape ice from windshields are quite effective in getting rid of ice build-up.

Wash all removable parts in your sink and dry them thoroughly before returning to the freezer. Wipe the entire interior surface with baking soda; never use cleansers, as they will dull the appliance finish.

This is also a good time to move your freezer so you can vacuum around, behind, and under it. Dust which has accumulated can cut down on appliance efficiency.

Care of your Dishwasher

Never go off and leave the dishwasher running. The temptation is great, I know, but not worth the chance you take. Every year numerous dishwashers malfunction (because some water sediment gets caught in the valve), and the surrounding area is flooded. Just imagine what would happen if you turned your faucet on full blast and let the water run on the floor until you returned. Needless to say, the damage is usually quite extensive, involving warped floors on the entire level of the building. Clean the screen or drain in the bottom of the dishwasher frequently to keep it working efficiently.

Cleaning Your Stove and Oven

According to surveys, oven cleaning is one of the most hated chores. If you feel this way, maybe you can draw straws in your family to see who will be the "lucky one." When buying a new stove, you should very seriously consider the automatic self-cleaning ovens (not to be confused with continuous-cleaning ovens).

Follow the manufacturer's directions when you use oven cleaner. (Soak drip pans in bleach or ammonia solution overnight.)

Once your stove top and oven are cleaned, remember that prevention is the easiest of all cleaners. Use heavy foil liner for the bottom of your oven if you wish. Avoid spillovers while baking by placing baking utensils on a cookie sheet or a foil pan to catch anything that might bubble over. Wipe spills up as soon as they occur. Good daily and weekly maintenance can postpone major cleaning. Stainless steel or enamel stove top drip pans are easiest to clean and well worth the extra money for replacements if you don't already have them.

CLEANING SCORCHED PANS. This method should not be used on Teflon pans, but works magic on Pyrex, glass, porcelain and all types of metal pans. Fill your scorched container with one part household bleach to four parts water. Simmer over low heat or, if container is not flame proof, place in slow oven until all burnt matter has dissolved and loosened. Or you may use one part bleach to one part water and let pan soak overnight. Either way, the pan will clean easily.

Insects in the Kitchen

Having "creepy crawlers" in the kitchen does not necessarily mean that your housekeeping routine leaves something to be desired. It is possible that you have purchased food that was already infected. There are many kinds of moth larvae and beetles that attack cereal products, flour, rice, spaghetti, noodles, certain spices, dry dog food, popcorn, and garden seed. Flour beetles, saw-toothed grain bettles, flat grain bettles, carpet beetles, bean weevils, pea weevils, rice weevils, Indian meal moths, and Mediterranean flour moths are some of the more common ones. These insects can be found in packages or containers of dried plant food, as well as food products. Once they infest your cabinets or cupboards they can gain entrance to many unopened packages as well. Since most of them are capable of flying, they may enter the house that way also. However, their most usual entrance is through packaged food brought into the house. Once they get a foothold, they will spread to other foods and become progressively more abundant.

The best way to attack this problem is to do something about it as soon as you notice any food being infested. Throw out infested foods *immediately*. Store all packaged foods, open and unopened, from that particular cupboard in your freezer for a period of 72 hours. This will kill all stages of any insects that may be present.

If you have a bad infestation, remove all food, cooking utensils, and dishes from the cabinet area and apply a residual insecticide. Under no conditions allow the insecticide to come into direct contact with foods, cooking utensils, dishes, or food handling surfaces. Remove nearby foods and cover them carefully to avoid contamination. Do not replace foodstuff, cooking utensils, or dishes until the spray deposit has completely dried. Cupboards and drawers, such as silverware and utensil drawers, should have paper liners removed before spraying. Reline with clean paper before returning items to drawers and cupboards. Before using an insecticide, read the label carefully and follow directions. For severe or repeated infestation, call an exterminator.

GETTING RID OF THE CLUTTER

Knickknacks

Housekeeping and home maintenance time can be cut considerably if you get rid of the clutter. Take a critical view of your home. Are the table tops and shelves in your living quarters covered with "little doodads"? Do you have little knickknacks everywhere that require constant dusting? If so, see what things can be removed without giving your room a bare or stark look. Most people will be amazed at the number of appointments sitting around that really do not add to the total decorating effect they are trying to achieve. If you are a collector, put these items behind glass so they won't need constant attention, or pack them away until such a time that you can properly take care of them. You don't want to spend all your spare time dusting and cleaning. Remember the old adage "less is more."

Closets, Shelves, Drawers

Also take a very critical look at your closets and shelves. How many things do you have there that you really don't need or use, but don't wish to throw away? A garage sale may be the answer to your problem. It is a fun way of getting rid of lots of things while realizing a profit. One family I know was going to put their house up for sale and move into a larger home, simply because they found their home too "crowded." In order to get ready for the move and to get their house in shape for selling, they went through every room, closet by closet, shelf by shelf, drawer by drawer, eliminating all but those things that they really needed and used. All the superfluous items were offered at the garage sale. When the sale was over, the occupants found that they really did have sufficient room in their present home. The money they earned from the garage sale was substantial, and naturally, the house was much easier to care for in its uncluttered state.

If you work full time it may even be worthwhile spending part of your vacation to do this. One woman I know takes off a day or two during the middle of the week when no one is home. This leaves her to go through drawers and closets undisturbed. If you happen to be a saver, discarding may be a very difficult thing to do, but force yourself. You'll find the dividends large and worthwhile.

The Children's Rooms

Children's rooms can be a big bugaboo. Most children have a tendency to collect stones, shells, marbles, odd pieces of games—the list is unending. If you can't talk them into getting rid of their "collections," at least pack them away and put them in a storage locker, attic, or garage. Get them out of the house. You'll be amazed at how much quicker and easier your housekeeping chores, as well as theirs, will be with this new look.

The Kitchen

Do the same thing with your kitchen. Do you have pans, trays, and other serving items that you never use? Pack them away in a carton, and if you don't need any of the things within a year or two, get rid of them. Yes, this may include odd wedding gifts and other sentimental things that you really don't wish to part with. If things that have real sentimental value, either resign yourself to using them or pack them away for safekeeping. You can always rationalize when you sell or give away things, such as to a rummage sale or thrift shop, that you are recycling these items and will give someone else the opportunity of using them (which you obviously have not done).

Here again, an uncluttered kitchen is much easier to maintain than one that is completely "filled." Junk drawers are the most rewarding of all to go through. You'll find, if you are the typical homemaker, all sorts of assorted items that may have been in the drawer for years— odd screws, nails, pieces of string, broken-down ball-point pens, old recipe clippings, and other memorabilia. Read over the recipes and determine if you really wish to keep them. Put those you wish to keep in an envelope or file folders properly labeled, so that you can find them when needed. You'll be amazed at what a wonderful sense of accomplishment all this will give you.

SYMBOLS

A frequent remark I hear is, "I never use my microwave oven (food processor, blender, or whatever)..." For your convenience, the symbols below appear throughout this book to encourage you to use these appliances if you have them. However, these recipes can be made in the conventional manner. You'll find the appliance symbol located directly across from the ingredients or instructions where it would be useful. Be sure to check manufacturer's directions for specific instructions on appliance use.

This symbol indicates that the recipe can be adapted to your microwave oven. Units vary, so refer to your manufacturer's manual for detailed instructions. The microwave symbols are a reminder for those of you who have a microwave oven to use it to its fullest advantage.

This symbol means a food processor can be used to slice, grate, shred, chop, grind, mix or perform other time-consuming operations.

This symbol indicates that a recipe is easily adapted for a slow cooker. See manufacturer's instructions for specifics.

Bearing this symbol are pantry recipes, which can be used on those occasions when you haven't been able to go shopping and need to put a quick meal together. The ingredients can be stored for a long period of time on your pantry shelf or in your freezer. Keep the ingredients for a few of these recipes on hand and you'll never be caught without a quick meal "up your sleeve."

This symbol indicates recipes that are great to fix ahead and serve later. Often, you may want to eat shortly after you walk in the door with little or no effort on your part. Soups and one-pot meals made in a slow cooker are just right for these occasions, along with numerous other fix-ahead recipes. The preparation needn't be involved or lengthy. For example, most slow cooker recipes can be put together in 5 minutes, simmered all day and served that evening with little or no extra work needed at serving time. In this book you will find many recipes that also lend themselves well to entertaining. On those occasions, you don't want to have a lot of last-minute preparation. These fix-ahead recipes also lend themselves well to busy weekends. Preparation for many of these recipes can be made a day or more in advance if necessary.

You will find a timer symbol on all recipes that can be made in 20 minutes or less. When you are in a hurry, just look for the timer.

EQUIPPING YOUR KITCHEN

With all the marvelous appliances, large and small, available to today's homemaker, only you can decide which appliance will serve you best. Consider your needs, your type of cooking, and your own personal preferences. I had one mother tell me that she would never consider getting a dishwasher; she talks with each of her children as they dry or wash the dishes along with her. This is their time to communicate in a casual, relaxed manner and discuss problems. Myself, I have anxiety attacks if the dishwasher even sounds as though it might not make it through the week. (We can "talk" some other time, some other place!)

Some people couldn't live without a slow cooker, and yet there are others I have talked to who have them sitting on a shelf and never use them. You don't want to clutter up your house or waste your money on appliances that you are not going to use. Give each appliance serious thought before purchasing it. Because of individual differences of personality and life-style, I will attempt to mention all the advantages and, in some cases, disadvantages of the various appliances, so you can decide whether these appliances are for you.

Are you willing to learn new things? Will you take the time to read the instructions thoroughly? With many of the new appliances, especially the microwave oven, this is most important. Courses are being offered in many local adult education classes held in the evening, as well as at private cooking schools, on how to use the microwave oven and the food processor. If you're not good at reading and following instructions, perhaps attending some of these classes is for you. You may even wish to attend one before purchasing the appliance. Most stores offer periodic demonstrations where you can see the units used; these should also help you determine whether that particular appliance is for you.

Once your kitchen is conveniently arranged, the next step is to plan the proper equipment. A cabinetmaker cannot build a beautiful cabinet efficiently without the proper tools. Neither can a cook operate efficiently without the proper equipment. Just as no two craftsmen would probably agree on which tools to buy, no two cooks would have the same ideas about what equipment is essential. I shall try to list some of the things that I find helpful, as well as those that I find indispensable. You'll have to decide for yourself which utensils to add to your own kitchen.

You must thoroughly evaluate the type of cooking you do and the type of equipment you really will use. Otherwise, you can end up having your shelves, cabinets, and counter space cluttered with supplies a French chef might envy, but that you seldom or never use.

Before you add any new equipment to your kitchen, it is a good idea to go over the appliances you already have on hand. If you have equipment or appliances you rarely use, pack them away (unless you have unlimited storage space in your kitchen), or better yet, donate them to some thrift shop.

Utensils and Gadgets

The following is a list of basic equipment necessary to cook efficiently. Having several sets of measuring cups and spoons and spatulas will eliminate having to stop and wash utensils during meal preparation: baster, kitchen shears, bottle opener, can opener, collander, corkscrew, grater, juicer, meat thermometer, wide and narrow metal and rubber spatulas (several), a graduated set of metal mixing bowls (also glass if you have a microwave oven), wooden spoons, tongs, standard measuring cups for dry measure, glass measuring cups in variety of sizes for liquid measuring, measuring spoons (several sets), strainer, wire whisk, good set of cutlery knives, garlic press, wooden cutting board, knife sharpener, potato peeler.

Use drawer dividers, special racks, or holders to make tools and gadgets easy to find and to keep them from becoming bent, dented, or broken. An attractive crock or ceramic container is very convenient for holding things such as spatulas, wooden spoons, and wire whisks near your stove, while taking up very little counter space. Pegboard on a wall and a magnetic knife holder can also accommodate some of your smaller utensils.

Dishwashers

Anyone cooking for three or more people should put a dishwasher at the head of the list of things to acquire. With the vast array of models now available—and there will be more to come—only those women with the tiniest of kitchens would have trouble finding a small niche for this most useful appliance. You're really not up on things if you still have the notion that dishes have to be rinsed almost clean before putting them into the dishwasher, or that dishwashers are more trouble than washing by hand, and so on. I could easily write several paragraphs on the virtues of having a dishwasher and how different life has been since we got ours. According to American Home Appliance Manufacturers, a dishwasher saves the average household 1 hour a day in dishwashing chores. That's 365 hours a year, or nine 40-hour weeks a year! Those figures explain why I put this appliance at the top of the list! A dishwasher represents a considerable energy savings as well. If it is run only once a day, it uses less water than washing dishes by hand three times a day.

Freezers

Inadequate refrigerator or freezer storage space is a serious handicap. It will involve extra trips to the grocery store. If it's your own refrigerator or freezer that's inadequate, a new one may be a good investment. However, if you are renting, perhaps a small portable freezer would suffice. Having adequate freezer space will allow you to shop less frequently, cook less frequently, save money when shopping by buying specials in large quantities, and entertain at a moment's notice. Even a small freezer in a refrigerator, when used properly, can be a very big help in saving you kitchen drudgery. When I speak of a small compartment in a refrigerator, I mean the two-door freezer-refrigerator combination. The older type refrigerators that have an ice cube storage section are really not adequate for freezing. Please don't keep anything more than a week or two at most in this type of unit.

TEMPERATURE. In order to preserve food properly, your freezer should maintain a temperature of zero degrees Fahrenheit. Anything above that will cause loss of flavor and deterioration of nutrition and quality of the food. Please remember that water freezes at 32 degrees Fahrenheit, and from outward appearances your food may seem to be solidly frozen, but the process of deterioration will continue unless your food is held at zero degrees. The only way to determine this is to have a thermometer in your freezer. Keep your freezer control at the coldest setting. It is best to err on the side of safety. A colder freezer will not harm your food but will freeze your food more quickly when stored there.

PLACEMENT. Freezers may be stored in garages, basements, utility rooms, or porches. Where space is limited, the small chest-type freezer with a butcher block top may be most convenient. This small unit can be purchased on casters, so that you may move it around in your kitchen as needed. Only a small percentage of people who have this marvelous appliance, the freezer, use it to its fullest advantage. (This author's newly revised *The Freezer Cookbook,* also published by Contemporary Books, Inc., is filled with time saving ideas for the freezer owner.)

Most people seem to think a freezer is only for those with large families or people living on a farm who have a lot of produce to freeze. This simply isn't true; a freezer is just as vital for the person living alone. Anyone who has ever tried cooking for one or two people knows the problems involved. If you have a taste for baked ham, for example, you face the dilemma of eating ham for a week or not having it at all. A large family doesn't have this problem; neither does the person with a freezer. Have the butcher cut a steak from either the butt or shank end of a ham, wrap it, and freeze it for future broiling. After the first meal of baked ham, you can slice some of the meat for sandwiches, make a small ham and scalloped potato casserole, ham and bean soup (see page 76), and so on. The possibilities are unlimited. The very same may be done with most cuts of meat and poultry, especially turkey, as well as pastries, cake, and vegetable dishes.

FOOD ROTATION. The most efficient way to use your freezer is to rotate your food frequently. Do not keep food in the freezer indefinitely. Always freezer-wrap your food carefully, then date and label it. The more food you have in and out of your freezer in a given period of time (say a week or a month), the more service you are getting from your freezer. If you have a frost-free freezer, which doesn't need periodic defrosting, it is expecially easy to "lose" food in the back or bottom recesses of your freezer, particularly if it is large. Try to avoid this by periodically rearranging and straightening out your freezer and checking its corners. Unplug your freezer before cleaning it; wet hands can easily be frozen to the metal surfaces of a freezer. It's best to wear gloves.

Food Processors

The Cuisinart Food Processor was first introduced in the United States in 1973, but sales didn't take off until 1975. It was instant love from the first time I used this marvelous machine. The food processor was designed to liberate the cook. It eliminated the drudgery of preparing and cooking food. One could hardly wait for the next meal to chop, grate, slice, or mix with this marvelous new "toy." Dishes that were formerly reserved only for special occasions could now be prepared in a "wink." Rich brown onion soups are made with nary a tear; potato pancakes could be made and fingernails would still be intact. Coleslaw, marinated cucumbers, and myriad vegetable dishes that you know are good for you but often don't have the time to prepare become real quickie dishes. Needless to say, the love affair has lasted these several years. If I had to eliminate all my appliances except one (other than my dishwasher and freezer), that one would be the food processor.

Strangely enough, the Cuisinart Food Processor was on the market for several years before appliance manufacturers took this product seriously. It was primarily considered a novelty, with only a very limited market in the U.S. When sales started soaring, appliance manufacturers took another look at this machine, and suddenly everyone and his grandfather had a food processor of some sort available. During the winter Housewares Show in 1978, there were no less than 15 food processors on the market.

I am constantly asked which of the less expensive machines is the best. Because prices range from $50 to $250 (at the time of publication), this is not a simple question to answer. We have spent a great deal of time testing the various food processors reviewed here and we'll try to give an honest and objective evaluation of each machine as it performed for us. You will have to decide which machine is best suited to your needs and pocketbook. The food processor has done more to liberate the cook from drudgery than anything since the elimination of the woodburning stove.

American Gourmet® 8000 GK

Features: 350 watts; one-year motor warranty; brake; manual thermal overload set; interlock switch; liquid capacity, 28 ounces; dry capacity, 2 quarts; weighs 17 pounds; suggested retail price $69.95 (I have seen it discounted at $39); four blades (mixing, chopping, slicing, shredding); caddy for seven-blade storage.

Comments: 35-page recipe booklet. Counter stability fair. Cover was difficult to release: we experienced great difficulty with this during our testing and evaluation. Slicing blades for thin and thick didn't differ much. It sliced carrots and mushrooms poorly. Turning on and off was very hard. Noise level was loud.

Cuisinart® CFP5, CFP9

Features: 720 watts; one-year motor warranty; thermal overload set; circuit breaker; interlock switch; four blades (mixing, chopping, slicing, shredding); liquid capacity, 28 ounces; dry capacity, 2 quarts; CFP5 weighs 18 pounds, CFP9 weighs 15 pounds; suggested retail price CFP5—$200, CFP9—$140.

Comments: Very quiet; excellent counter stability. Recipe booklet includes 37 recipes (excellent). Sliced mushrooms adequately with medium and fine blades, although there were more small pieces than with some of the other food processors. Pusher fits either way, which is a great convenience. Chops, slices and grates cheeses and vegetables beautifully. Does not "walk" when working. Chops meat to perfection. Blends pastry dough in seconds. Small amounts of yeast dough can be quickly and smoothly mixed. Good blending action, although one must be careful about adding too much liquid—it might "leak" out the bottom. Extra accessories available.

Cuisinart Model DLC-7—See Addendum, page 190.

Farberware Food Processor

Features: 315 watts; 1-year motor warranty; brake; automatic thermal overload set; automatic circuit breaker; interlock switch; on/off switch; capacity, 28 oz., liquid; 2 qt dry; weighs 16½ lbs.; national service centers; suggested retail price $120; 4 blades (mix, chop, shred, slice); tube cover (locking tabs, activating cam).

Comments: Blades have easy-grip handles. Use and recipe guide (64 recipes). Pastry dough blended well with plastic blade. Excellent slicing disc for mushrooms, carrots and other vegetables; chopped very finely and evenly. Grated cheese very nicely. Food pusher fits in only one way—inconvenient if you sit it down and have to use it again. Mixed yeast dough very quickly and thoroughly. Moderately quiet. Extra accessories available.

Hamilton Beach Food Processor

Features: 330 watts; one-year motor warranty; liquid capacity, 32 ounces; dry capacity, 2.1 quarts; weighs 12 pounds; national service centers; suggested retail price $159.95; four blades (cutting, shredding, slicing, mixing); brake; automatic thermal overload set; exclusive double interlock switch (on/off switch controls power even when container is locked to go).

Comments: Moderately quiet. Use and recipe guide book (55 pages). Metal blade worked very well for piecrust dough. Plastic blade worked equally well for cookie dough. Grated hard and soft cheese with very acceptable results. Slicing blade produced uniform mushroom slices. Symbols on the front of the machine indicate which blade to use for each recipe.

La Machine™ by Moulinex

Features: 590 watts; one-year motor warranty; automatic thermal overload set; interlock switch; on/off switch; liquid capacity, 5 cups; dry capacity, 1 quart, weighs 11½ pounds; suggested retail price $119.95; four blades (cutting, chopping, slicing, shredding).

Comments: No large bowl, included only 1-quart bowl for chopping. Continuous processing. Operating manual excellent and attractive (22 recipes). Moderately quiet. Food pusher fits in only one way, which is annoying; cutting blade locks in place and is removed with a special tool. On/off control is spring loaded for instant stopping of motor and cutting blade (no circuit breaker needed). This is a nice safety feature, because the cutting blades will not continue twirling around when you remove the lid. Mushrooms and carrots were sliced uniformly. Chopping blade threw mushrooms to side of bowl, had to stop machine to scrape bowl several times. Chopped olives and nuts in the small bowl container; did a good job. Extra accessories available.

Le Chef™ by Sunbeam®

Features: 600 watts; one-year warranty; brake; automatic thermal overload set; interlock switch; on/off switch; circuit breaker liquid capacity, 37 ounces; dry capacity, 2.5 quarts; weighs 15 pounds; national service centers; suggested retail price $139.95; four blades (cutting/processing, mixing, shredding, slicing).

Comments: Well-written recipe and instruction booklet (62 pages). Moderately quiet. Sliced mushrooms poorly. Works fine with all-purpose cutting/processing blade, on-and-off pulsating. Chopped cabbage uniformly. Grating was fine, almost too fine for some things. Food pusher doubles as a measuring cup with ounces and metric measurements. Extra accessories available.

New Ronic by Bon Jour Imports

Features: 160–300 watts; lifetime warranty; safety brake motor; automatic thermal overload set; interlock switch; liquid capacity, 30 ounces; dry capacity, 45 ounces; suggested retail price $129.50; three blades (chopping/julienne, slicing, chopping/mixing).

Comments: Rounded bowls for dual action mixing and chopping. Recipe and instruction booklet. The slicing blade chopped most vegetables more than it sliced; however, celery was satisfactory. The feeding tube pusher fit in only one way. Blades are aluminum instead of stainless steel. It didn't blend or mix liquids and solids as well as some of the other food processors. This machine has two tops, one with feeder tube, one without. Very quiet. The rubber gripper insets on base of machine came out (they're not attached very securely) and, consequently, the machine walked all over the counter. Made yeast dough very satisfactorily. Removing the metal blade was very difficult when wet or slippery with dough on it because there is no gripper.

Omnichef™ by Cuisinart®

Features: 350 watts; one-year motor warranty; interlock switch; circuit breaker; liquid capacity, 32 ounces; dry capacity, 2.1 quarts; weighs 12 pounds; suggested retail price $120; three blades (chopping, slicing, grating).

Comments: Work bowl cover activates the motor. No gripper when removing chopping blade—if hands were wet or oily, it would be impossible to remove blades. Circuit breaker turned off motor with less than 4 ounces of cheese to grate. Bowl has a screw-type lock and there's no indication on the bowl as to which way to turn it. It is difficult to lock in place and you must be very careful to get it on evenly. Slicing blade is very difficult to remove; it sets down in work bowl with no handle or knob to remove it. Mushrooms were more chopped than sliced. Grated soft cheese very nicely. Machine is quiet when in operation. Good recipe booklet (186 pages).

Toastmaster® by McGraw-Edison

Features: 600 watts; one-year motor warranty; on/off pulsating switch; overload protection circuit breaker; liquid capacity, 33 ounces; dry capacity, 2 quarts; weighs 18 pounds; suggested retail price, $79.95; four blades (mixing/kneading, chopping, slicing, shredding).

Comments: Moderately quiet. When chopping cabbage, some of the cabbage was pulverized by the time the rest was chopped. Grating blade works fine, but is a little coarse (too coarse for potato pancakes). Slicing was average for mushrooms. Instruction and recipe booklet (58 pages) had a recipe for Chicken Puffs that sounded great, but it didn't work.

Waring Food Processor

Features: 860 watts; lifetime warranty; brake; automatic thermal overload set; interlock switch; on/off switch; liquid capacity, 38 ounces; dry capacity, 2.5 quarts; weighs 19 pounds; national service centers; suggested retail price $180; four blades (chopping, slicing, shredding, mixing); tool caddy for accessory discs and adapter.

Comments: Tandem blade action allows both the cutting blade and a processing disc to be used together. You can slice and chop or shred and mix at the same time. A nice feature, but one you probably won't use that much. Quiet motor. Instruction and recipe booklet (23 pages). Slicing blade sliced vegetables evenly and uniformly. Pastry dough was blended quickly, cheese and cabbage shredded uniformly. Has new attachment for whipping egg whites and cream. Will not whip to full volume as with beaters, but nice feature to have when in a hurry. The motor and cutting tool will come to a rapid stop (within 2–3 seconds), because of the special electrical circuitry. The clear plastic food pusher with English and metric markings doubles as a convenient 8-ounce (240ml) measuring cup. Extra accessories available.

Multi-Purpose Kitchen Centers

The machines discussed in this section are multi-use appliances: primarily electric mixers with a variety of attachments and/or accessories to grate, grind, chop, slice and sometimes blend, as well as perform a variety of other chores. If you don't have a stationary mixer and do quite a bit of baking, you may wish to consider one of these machines. Where counter space is not limited, both a kitchen center and food processor may be considered.

Yeast dough made in a food processor is generally not as finely textured or as moist as dough kneaded in the traditional manner. Creaming butter and sugar until light and fluffy or whipping cream and egg whites are best done with a mixer. It is also difficult, if not impossible, to fold fruits such as blueberries into a mixture in a food processor without getting the berries all chopped up.

When considering a food processor versus a multi-purpose kitchen center, remember that only small quantities of yeast or regular dough can be mixed at one time in a food processor. Mixers are different from food processors and do not have the capabilities of making light, fluffy pastry dough in 30 seconds, as well as other chopping action.

There is no one machine that will do all your kitchen chores best; only you can decide which machine or machines will best suit your style and type of cooking.

Blakeslee Kitchen Machine A515MB, 1717MB

Features: 600 watts; one-year warranty; bowl capacity—5 and 7 quarts; three beaters (whisk, beater, dough hook); thick and fine slicers, medium coarse, and fine shredding blades, ice chipper; meat-chopping blades; high-speed and low-speed grating and slicing attachments; suggested retail price A515MB—$276, 1717MB—$315; on/off switch.

Comments: Instruction booklet (27 pages). Aesthetically probably the most attractive machine, it has a very slick and sculptured look. When the speed is increased, the noise volume also increases. Unfortunately, at the highest speed it is quite noisy. Machine has a lot of power and works very well with its attachments. Both high-speed and low-speed grating and slicing attachments did a commendable job of slicing and grating vegetables and cheeses.

One convenience of the Blakeslee is that the power rises with the push of a button, allowing easy access to the mixing bowl when adding additional ingredients or scraping down the sides of the bowl. Wire whisk mixing attachment is small in size compared to others and took twice as long to beat egg whites as the KitchenAid wire whisk. Yeast dough was kneaded very satisfactorily, as were batter doughs. Attachments are all dishwasher proof and are very easy to connect and use. Extra accessories available for the Blakeslee are a blender, sausage maker, colander and sieve, juice extractor, cream maker, coffee grinder, bean slicer–pea huller, can opener, and potato peeler.

Braun Kitchen Machine

Features: 400 watts; one-year warranty; suggested retail price $160; capacity—1 large bowl (14 cups), 1 small bowl (suitable for up to 6 egg whites, 1½ cups whipping cream, or 2½–3 cups thick mixture); five blades (grating, two shredding, thick and thin slicing) and disc holder; whisk and dough hook for mixer.

Comments: Machine is moderately noisy. Drive arm to attach whisk and dough hook has identifying sockets for appropriate hook. Must remove drive arm to insert hooks before placing bowl on pin. Dough hook didn't work too well in making yeast dough. Dough was lumpy, so had to insert whisk to beat it smooth and then removed whisk and inserted dough hook again. This can be messy and a waste of time. Small bowl is great, but ingredients settle in groove at bottom of bowl where pin is set.

The blades worked very well. Grating cheese on the three types of blades gives a nice variety of textures; the same is true with cabbage for coleslaw and other vegetables. Mushrooms sliced with either thick or thin blade were nice and uniform, as were carrots and other vegetables. Grated almonds well on fine grater. The 127-page spiral-bound instruction book is well written and nicely illustrated. Symbols are used with each recipe, indicating which attachment and/or blade should be used. Extra accessories are juicer, meat grinder, blender, coffee grinder.

KitchenAid® K5A, K45

Features: 300 watts; one-year warranty; on/off switch; speed control lever; mixer with flat beater, wire whip, dough hook; bowl capacity, 5 quarts (K5A), 4½ quarts (K45); suggested retail price K5A—$229.95, K45—$169.95.

Comments: Recipe and instruction booklet included (49 pages). The K5A head does not raise up and back as it does with the smaller model; consequently, adding ingredients and stirring down sides of bowl is more difficult. Both models work extremely well for their primary purpose as electric mixers. Motor strong and quiet. Whipping beater is great for whipping cream and egg whites to full volume. The pouring shield which fits both models is a marvelous invention. It allows you to add dry ingredients when the mixer is in motion without splattering. It also can be used as a shield to keep items such as whipping cream from splashing about at high speed.

The DVS-disc vegetable slicer, which operates on both models, comes with three different blades—fine, coarse, and ice chopping. It does its job well; however, it's an enormous piece of equipment that not only takes up a lot of storage room, but also takes up a good part of the dishwasher when washing it. The food grinder and sausage stuffer work reasonably well. The beater shaft continues to rotate all the time machine is in motion, even when using slicing and grating attachments. This can be very annoying, as it will knock down the bowl which you are trying to fill with the shredded food.

Extra accessories that can be purchased and used with the KitchenAid appliance are can opener, grain mill, silver buffer, food grinder (coarse and fine plate); slicer, shredder (rotor type with four cones, fine shredder, coarse shredder and shoe stringer, thick slicer, thin slicer); juice extractor; fine and coarse ice-chipping plates; automatic colander and sieve.

Oster Kitchen Center

Features: 300 watts; one-year warranty; bowl capacity—4 quarts and 1½ quarts; mixer has dough hooks and regular beaters; food grinder has fine and coarse grinding discs; Food Crafter has four blades (slicing, shredding, thick/thin slicing, French fry cutter); blender has 5-cup glass container; suggested retail price, $179.95.

Comments: Recipe booklet included (112 pages). The Food Crafter grater for cheese was great. Slicing blades (thick and thin) were uniform on mushrooms and water chestnuts. Green peppers sliced well. You cannot chop meat with the Food Crafter, you must use the grinder attachment. The slicing blade did not slice meat at all—it shredded it! Food pusher goes in only one way. Glass mixing bowls (there are two sizes, which is most convenient) are great if you have or are planning to get a microwave oven. You can melt shortening, heat liquid for yeast dough, etc., right in your mixing bowl.

Doughmaker hooks are designed so that they beat slower; the mixing ability of this machine does not compare with Braun, Kitchen-Aid, or Blakeslee. The eggs floated to the top of the batter and slipped through beaters repeatedly. The mixer does lift up to release beaters or scrape batter. If you're not careful when raising the beaters, you could easily disconnect the whole mixer. The grinder ground ham salad smoothly and uniformly. Extra accessories are available.

3600 Dome Lid Vita Mix® with Spigot

Features: 225 rpm blade tip speed; capacity varies, depending upon what you're making; five-year warranty; weighs 16 pounds; suggested retail price $249.95.

Comments: A very complicated machine to operate. Must use their yeast dough recipes, cannot adapt other bread and yeast dough recipes. Our first attempt at mixing bread dough was disastrous, until we found out you cannot use your own recipe. The machine started smoking with the ingredients in the container, and there was no circuit breaker to counteract this process. It is not a juicer, as indicated; it does not extract juice from pulp. It actually pulverizes ingredients if sufficient liquid is added. The pressurized spigot didn't work well, either. The instruction booklet is very poorly organized. Machine doesn't come apart for easy cleaning and is not dishwasher safe.

Sunbeam Food Preparation Center—see Addendum, page 190.

Microwave Ovens

The microwave oven has been around for a long time but is just now coming into its own. Because of increased demand, prices have come down. They are still by no means cheap, but considering the convenience and the new improvements, the microwave oven is a fantastic asset for every cook, but especially for the busy cook. It can be a real lifesaver when you've neglected to thaw your dinner meat or casserole.

Frozen vegetables can be cooked right in the packages, eliminating the need to wash extra pots and pans. Baked potatoes are ready in just a few minutes—a special delight for the working person. Leftover meals never tasted so good and can be warmed right on your serving plate if you choose. (See Leftovers, page 37.) The microwave oven is especially nice when you are serving one or two meals at a time. Not only does it save you a lot of energy by eliminating the need to wash many pots and pans, but also it uses considerably less energy than a conventional stove or oven.

Not all microwave ovens have a defrost cycle on them; this is a marvelous feature which is certainly worth the extra cost. Temperature probes, which are new on microwave ovens, are another worthwhile feature to consider.

All microwave ovens come with a book of instructions. Read yours carefully. You will note that we indicate on our recipes where the microwave oven unit is applicable. This is a book about time-saving ideas and recipes for the busy person and our space is limited, so detailed instructions on microwave cooking are not possible. Please check your microwave oven instruction book for information on timing and other procedures. The microwave symbols are merely a reminder for those of you who have a microwave oven to use it to its fullest advantage.

General Electric's *The Microwave Guide and Cookbook* is beautifully illustrated and quite informative. I suggest you check your library for this marvelous book, as well as the numerous other microwave cookbooks now available.

ACCESSORIES. A browning skillet, a bacon cooker, and covered Pyrex dishes in an assortment of sizes are a few of the accessories you should acquire for your microwave cooking. A half gallon (8 cups) measure and 1 quart measuring cups are indispensable for measuring and making (in the same container) such things as puddings, custards, soups, gravies, and sauces. Having the proper accessories will increase your efficiency and enjoyment of microwave cooking. You may wish to invest in refrigerator-to-microwave-oven storage and cooking containers. Corning makes some containers with both plastic and glass lids. Use flat plastic stackable lids for refrigerator or freezer storage, and glass lids for microwave cooking.

Slow Cookers

Slow cookers are a relatively recent addition to the appliance market. They come in many types and sizes, and lend themselves perfectly to the needs of a person who is away from the house a good deal of the time. You can put your dinner on in the morning before you leave for work and have it ready for you when you come home at night.

The slow cookers that have heat coils around the sides, are made of stone, or have a stoneware insert generally work most effectively. There's less tendency to burn with this type slow cooker, and they use a minimum amount of water. I particularly like the ones with the insert that can be removed at serving time and placed in your dishwasher after use.

If you have a very long commuting distance or work an extra long day, you may wish to attach this slow cooker to an automatic timer. For example, if you leave the house at 7:00 A.M. and are not expected back until 6:30 P.M., your pot roast would pretty well be falling apart by the time you returned home. An alternative is to get an electric timer. Plug your slow cooker into this timer and have it go on at, say, 10:00 in the morning. If your meat was very cold or partially frozen, this would work out satisfactorily. By the way, these electric timers have many other advantages—you can make your coffee the night before; plug in your appliance so that your coffee is piping hot and ready when you awaken the next morning. You may also use them to turn lights off and on when you are on vacation or away for an extended period.

Select the size of the slow cooker you purchase carefully. Slow cookers work more effectively when they are two-thirds filled. In other words, a 5-quart slow cooker will not work effectively with 2 quarts of food in it.

Be sure to read your instruction and recipe book carefully. You may also wish to supplement this information with a slow cooker cookbook or two; there are many good ones on the market. We have included for your convenience a slow cooker symbol which will be placed by all the recipes that lend themselves well to slow cooking.

Electric Mixers

A stationary electric mixer should be high on your list of kitchen appliances if you do a lot of baking. Portables are handy for some jobs, but they simply don't take the place of a stationary mixer. If you have a food processor, perhaps a portable is all that you need, especially if you do only a minimum amount of baking. While the food processor will do many things, it will not whip egg whites as well as a mixer or cream butter and shortening until it's light and fluffy, as required in some recipes. You can mix yeast dough in a food processor, but only in very small portions. (The DLG-7 Cuisinart model is the only food processor that will knead 3 pounds of bread at one time.

Stainless steel electric mixers are slightly more expensive, but worth every additional cent. You'll never have to worry about chipping paint or staining. Moreover, the stainless steel bowls that come with these mixers have a larger capacity than the glass bowls. The stainless steel bowls of some models hold as much as 1 quart more than their glass counterparts. This makes an enormous difference when you are mixing large quantities of any recipe.

If you're thinking of buying a new mixer, it might be well to consider the larger, more expensive models that come with bread hooks. See our evaluation on page 30. Making yeast dough with one of these machines is such fun! It isn't necessary to knead your dough at all, and your mixing time is cut in half. Even if you've never done so before, you'll be tempted to make breads and coffee cakes on a regular basis.

Broiler Toasters

Until our toaster suddenly "died" this past year, I never gave this handy appliance too much thought. Now that I have one, I'm sorry that our toaster didn't meet its ill fate years ago. Not only does this unit do what an ordinary toaster does, but also it has the advantage of making toasted cheese sandwiches in an instant. You don't have to worry that the bagels are going to get stuck in the middle or that the thin-sliced rye is going to fall through the coils. Perfect for toasting almonds and sesame seeds without heating up your whole oven, it is also perfect for one or two lamb chops or heating a TV dinner. A broiler toaster would make a particularly nice gift for anyone living alone.

Blenders

If you don't have a food processor, I feel a blender is most vital. Do you have room to store it on your kitchen counter? A blender kept on the bottom of your kitchen cabinets won't be used often. Even though we have a food processor, we prefer using the blender for puréeing a large amount of vegetables when making soups and sauces, and for mixing juices, blender breakfasts, egg nogs, and malts, as well as frozen daiquiris and other such delights. I also like the mini-blender jars for mixing sauces and salad dressings and storing the leftovers right in the jar. These jars can be put back on the blender for a quick "stir" before using in the event that your sauce or dressing has settled somewhat during the storage period.

Multiplying Recipes

The recipes in this book are sometimes given in several different quantities so that they're adaptable to households of varying sizes. The person living alone will find the single quantities more suitable. Those with large families and large freezers will find the large quantities more to their liking. However, if you have a very large family, you may want to double or even multiply the larger quantities. Because space is limited, it isn't possible for one book to be all inclusive; each reader must determine how these recipes can best be used to suit his or her individual needs. When you multiply any recipes, it is best to take a minute and write down the quantity of each ingredient (write on the recipe itself if there is sufficient space) to avoid error. A common cause of failure in large-quantity cooking is that somewhere along the line the cook was distracted and didn't add the right proportion of ingredients. This can easily be avoided by just jotting them down. It will save time the next time you prepare it also.

IDEAS TO RELIEVE MORNING CHAOS

Every household will have to develop its own special morning routine. If at all possible, even though everyone leaves the house at a different time, try to serve breakfast at one seating. This saves a lot of wear and tear on the cook. Setting the breakfast table the night before also helps keep things running smoothly. This is another job that can easily be delegated.

If your family likes buttered toast for breakfast, keep just one stick of butter (or margarine) for this purpose. Tear the wrapper back a little bit and run it across the bread immediately after removing it from the toaster. The heat of the bread will melt the butter and you will have a smooth coat over the entire slice. No messy fingers, no crumbs in the butter dish. Quick as a wink.

Make your frozen orange juice in the blender, so you don't need to worry about thawing. Let everyone serve themselves right from the blender container. Blender breakfasts (see pages 44 through 46) can be a real timesaver.

Another time-saving idea is to have everyone remove his or her own plate, silverware, glasses, cups and saucers, rinse them, and put them in the dishwasher or kitchen sink. If you don't have a dishwasher, fill the sink with hot sudsy water and soak the dishes until it's convenient for someone to wash them. Although it isn't easy to start these routines, you'll be amazed at how habit-forming and automatic they become after awhile. It may seem like years of harping, reminding, and nagging "Don't forget to put your plate in the dishwasher," but in due time it will be done without conscious effort.

If you are continuously late and rushed in the morning, set your alarm for 15 minutes earlier. In your own mind, at least, decide on what you are going to serve for breakfast the night before. This will avoid taxing your foggy mind early in the morning. If that doesn't work, write it down. Remember, sweet rolls and milk do not constitute a well balanced breakfast.

Perhaps it would suit you best to get up a half-hour earlier, rather than face a messy kitchen and unmade beds at the end of the day. A rule I have always maintained is no one leaves the house without making his or her bed first! Somehow, no matter how much dust has accumulated, the house still seems in fairly decent order.

SERVING LEFTOVERS

There are several ways to handle this chronic problem. (1) Get a large dog. (2) If that doesn't appeal to you or your landlord, serve all the leftovers in your refrigerator at one time and call it a "smorgasbord." I know several families who do this regularly once a week. Either your family will enjoy this type of meal, or it will encourage them to finish everything on the table at each meal, eliminating the problem of leftovers. (3) Freeze the leftovers if there is enough for another whole meal. This isn't always possible. If you find you must serve the same dish twice in one week, serve it several days apart and plan an extra special dessert the second time around. I always feel a special dinner doesn't require much effort in the dessert department. Conversely, a simple meal, or especially a leftover dinner, is more appealing if the family knows a scrumptious dessert is to follow. A special dessert does not necessarily require a lot of time. You'll find many truly great desserts that are very easy to prepare in the Dessert section of this book.

Serving a bowl of soup beforehand will go a long way toward stretching a leftover meal. (See Soups, page 73.)

Refrigeration

Develop the habit of putting all leftovers in the refrigerator promptly after each meal. Be sure to store them covered. Hot foods should be reheated to at least 140°F. Remember that cold foods also harbor bacteria, particularly cream pies, custards, puddings, and egg and milk dishes. These leftovers should also be refrigerated immediately after each meal and kept refrigerated until just before serving. Check the inside of your refrigerator and make sure that it is maintained at a temperature of less than 40°F.

Reheating

Leftovers should look appealing and be served in an attractive manner. Proper heating and cooking techniques are important to preserve the flavor and nutritive value of the food without spoiling appearance and texture. Use low heat and heat to a serving temperature (140°F to 150°F). At this temperature bacteria have been killed, but vitamins and flavor have not been destroyed. Boiling and long cooking are not necessary and will usually spoil the flavor. Cover food when you are reheating it unless you want it to be crisp.

The microwave oven (see page 33) is a marvelous appliance for reheating leftovers. Vegetables, casseroles, meats, and other leftovers can be reheated and served right in their glass or ceramic refrigerator container. No additional water or liquid need be added, and you don't have to worry about the food sticking to the pan or about scorching it. If you don't have a microwave oven, use a double boiler; it's a good way of reheating many things, such as creamed dishes, stews, Stroganoffs, and prepared vegetables. You won't have to stand there stirring and pot-watching. Boil-in pouches make fine substitutes for a double boiler, particularly when you are heating several things at one time. Follow manufacturer's directions when using them. A thermostatically controlled heating unit on your stove is an ideal way for reheating some foods. Use a heavy, flat-bottomed pan the same size as your burner; do not use an oversized utensil. Spread the food evenly on the bottom and cover for slow, even heating. Most electrical appliances are thermostatically controlled and therefore are excellent for reheating foods. Your electric slow cooker, skillet, dutch oven, bean pot, wok, and steamer can all be used for heating leftovers.

Throughout this book you will find numerous recipes to use for such things as leftover ham, chicken, and other meats. In the beginning of the soup section there also is a part that gives you many ideas on using leftovers to make marvelous soups. With the price of food as expensive as it is today, nothing should be wasted. If you don't have time to prepare or use a leftover now, wrap it and put it in your freezer, properly marked, dated, and labeled for future use. Just as a restaurant chef never throws anything away, neither should you. Crepes are another marvelous way of using an assortment of leftover vegetables, seafood, and other dishes. Be innovative.

Mashed potatoes, with a little milk added, are great heated in plastic bags or double boiler. You can also add an egg, cheese, chives, and other seasonings and make potato patties. Baked potatoes, sliced and sautéed in vegetable oil at a high temperature until crispy, make marvelous hash browns.

Leftover or stale coffee cakes, cakes, and cookies can be turned into a marvelous dessert called gourmands (see page 167).

Make bread crumbs or croutons out of stale or leftover bread, toast, and heels of bread (if no one in your family likes these). Use these as buttered toppings for casseroles and vegetables and also add them to dishes such as meat loaf, or serve bread pudding (page 159) occasionally. Remember that whole-grained breads add more nutrition than do breads made from bleached white flour. If you are living in a small household that consumes very little bread, keep your bread in the freezer to keep it fresh and remove it as needed. It only takes a few minutes to thaw in the toaster.

To reheat rice spread it on a jelly roll pan (or for smaller amounts just a platter or pie plate), sprinkle with a little bit of water, and put it in your oven at 350°F, stirring every once in awhile. The rice will be ready to serve when it's piping hot. Leftover rice can also be used in puddings (see page 160).

Stale crackers, potato chips, corn chips, and other crunchies can sometimes be freshened up by placing in a 350°F oven for about 20 or 25 minutes. Also use as crumb toppings for casseroles or breading.

If you don't have a chance to finish your morning coffee, pour it into a glass container and refrigerate it before leaving. Reheat only to drinking temperature. Or if you have a good thermos pour the hot coffee into the thermos, and it will still be hot at dinner time.

Leftover meats, such as roast beef, pork roast, and turkey, are best sliced thinly and reheated in gravy. You may wish to remember this when cooking them the first time; be sure to save any juices or pan drippings that can be used for gravy. Be careful not to overcook.

TIPS ON ENTERTAINING

Having a party should be fun, and it can be if you follow some of the suggestions that have been shared with me by busy and working people who enjoy entertaining in a relaxed manner.

Table Setting

Set your table or buffet in a most attractive manner several days in advance, if that is convenient for you. If anything needs polishing or pressing, now is a good time to do it. When you're all finished, cover the table and buffet with a large plastic sheet that can be bought very inexpensively in your local hardware or paint supply store. These plastic sheets are sold as throwaway drop cloths and can be used over and over again.

At the same time get out all large serving pieces and appliances, making sure that each appliance has a cord and all the serving pieces are sparkling clean. If you find that you need to borrow something, make arrangements now. Having all these things done in advance will make you so much more relaxed at the time of your party. Try to use permanent press and soil-release tablecloths, cloth mats, and napkins. If this is not possible, cover your tablecloth near your punch bowl or other serving dish with a clear vinyl cloth. This may save you time in stain removal, and in ironing.

Meal Planning

Well in advance of the appointed day, dig out all of the recipes you will be using. Make up your shopping list and keep the recipes all clipped together in one place. Foods that can be made ahead of time and refrigerated or frozen should be first. When you have a spare "few minutes," you will want to prepare some of these in advance. Clipboards are great for keeping all your lists and recipes together, If you don't have one, seriously consider buying one or two.

Staples should be purchased way in advance, so that you're not exhausted with shopping and putting away all the nonperishable groceries and accessories, such as cocktail napkins and candles. Clean and polish all silverware and brass in advance (anyone can do this). Keeping your silver serving pieces wrapped in large plastic bags will help retard tarnishing, so that they will only need occasional attention. The contents of these plastic bags are also easily visible, so that you won't have to wrap and unwrap to see what's inside.

One hostess I know had paper cocktail and dinner napkins and disposable guest handtowels printed 100 at a time with "Betsy hates ironing." In white or colors you always use, I think it's a neat idea to copy and would make a lovely gift. Buy napkins or towels from restaurant suppliers and have the printing done at one of the small job-printing places popping up all over. They're usually quite inexpensive.

Breakfast and Brunch

Occasionally I read about a mother who wakes up before dawn, bakes bread, prepares 15 lunches, and does the family wash before breakfast. If this describes you, ignore this chapter; it isn't for you. We are mainly concerned here with the working person who has difficulty uttering any civilized sound before a second cup of coffee (which usually is had much later in the day). I'm in this group myself, and we need all the help we can get.

Some hints and recipe ideas follow to help you survive this part of the day.

NUTRITIONAL ADVANTAGES OF BREAKFAST

We've all heard it said many times that breakfast is the most important meal of the day. Certainly a large percentage of the population eats either no breakfast at all or the wrong type of breakfast, such as sweet rolls and coffee, tea, or milk. Remember, the body has gone without food for as long as 13, 14, or even 15 hours at breakfast time; for those who skip breakfast, the time between meals can often stretch to 17 hours. Studies have shown that people who do this (students as well as adults) are less alert and tend to become tired or sleepy as the day progresses, compared to those who had a satisfactory breakfast. A good breakfast should include milk or a dairy product; eggs, fish, or meat; juices or fruit; and some type of whole-grain cereal or bread.

Many nutritionists suggest that this meal should supply one-fourth to one-third of the recommended daily amounts of nutrients and calories. Dieting is often an excuse for missing breakfast; it is generally believed that food eaten earlier in the day is digested and expended in energy, while food eaten at the end of the day tends to be that which puts on weight. Study after study has shown that persons who eat an adequate breakfast turn out more work in the late morning, are more alert and quicker in their reactions, stand up better under stress, and do not tire as easily. With the help of convenient foods such as frozen juices (which can be mixed the night before), precooked ham and sausage patties, and quick-cooking and ready-to-eat cereals, a substantial breakfast can be put together very quickly. Keeping a good variety of breakfast ingredients on hand generally makes it easier for the cook and also adds more variety and interest to the meal.

Whole-grain breads toasted and spread with honey butter (see page 50), along with juice and milk, can be served in just minutes. Serve juice in a pitcher or blender top and let everyone serve themselves. Serve coffee and other hot beverages in mugs, which eliminates saucers—hence, fewer dishes. Use unsugared cereals and top them with sliced bananas for another quickie. On the following pages you will find recipes, including blender breakfasts, that can usually entice the most "unhungry" person.

Along with setting the table the night before, you might wish to put out boxes of cold cereal, distribute everyone's vitamins (if that is your routine), and have glasses ready to be filled with juice or milk. You'll be amazed at what a little planning the night before can do to change your morning atmosphere from frantic chaos to tolerable disorder.

Protein

Protein puts "strength" into your breakfast so you don't get hungry before your noon meal. Good breakfast protein foods are eggs, bacon, sausage, cheese, and peanut butter. All life requires protein, the chief tissue-builder in the body. Protein is made up of smaller units called amino acids, which number 18 or more. The amino acid makeup of a food determines its nutritive value. Proteins that supply all the essential amino acids in the same proportion they are needed by our body have the highest value. Generally they are foods of animal origin; meat, fish, poultry, eggs, and milk. Legumes, soy beans, and chick peas are almost as good a source of protein as animal sources; anyone following a vegetarian diet should eat plenty of them. Protein foods are essential in maintaining healthy muscles and fibroid tissue. They are also vital in the manufacture of hemoglobin, as well as antibodies which fight infection. Protein also supplies energy.

Bacon is best "fried" in the oven or microwave, a pound at a time, and put in freezer containers, ready to use for a quick breakfast. It may be left in strips or crumbled. For quick heating, use your microwave or a broiler-toaster unit. When cooking bacon in a microwave, cover with wax paper to avoid spattering.

Anyone who has ever burned bacon will enjoy the easier method of frying it in the oven. Put bacon in a single layer on top of your broiling pan and place it in a 400°F preheated oven. Bake for 10 to 15 minutes, depending on how crisp you want it. (This timing is for thin-sliced bacon; thicker slices will take longer.) There's no need to turn the bacon; it stays flat, and there seems to be much less shrinkage when it is cooked in this manner. Blot on absorbent towels.

Eggs have long been considered a breakfast staple. There are many simple ways of preparing them, including some of the recipes in this chapter, the easiest of which are blender breakfasts or breakfast-in-a-glass recipes. Plain soft-boiled eggs are often overlooked. You may wish to add them for variety. Eggs are a good meat substitute and should be included on your breakfast menu for variety.

Fruits and Juices

Fruits should be included on your daily breakfast menu; they include not only much-needed bulk and roughage, but also minerals and vitamins. Vitamin C is found in citrus fruits and juices, strawberries, bananas, pineapple, and melons. Vitamin A is found in cantaloupe, dried apricots, peaches, bananas (also a marvelous source of potassium), pineapple, pineapple juice, and dried prunes. Frozen juices, mixed the night before, are so convenient to serve, especially when fresh fruit is not available. Instead of cutting grapefruits in half and loosening all the segments with a grapefruit knife, try peeling it and serving just the grapefruit segments. Oranges may be peeled or cut in quarters and eaten as a finger food.

Bread and Cereals

For morning toast use whole-grain breads spread with butter, margarine, honey butter (see page 50), jams, jellies, or cheeses. These foods are excellent sources of energy and B vitamins, for healthy nerves and skin; they also promote normal digestion and appetite. Add extra nutrition to morning cereals by sprinkling a heaping tablespoon of wheat germ on a dish of cooked or dry cereal.

Milk and Milk Products

You can include this basic food group in your breakfast in several ways. Besides drinking milk, use cheese on your toast. Yogurts are becoming a very popular breakfast food. Milk is a source of calcium phosphate, which is necessary for healthy bones and teeth. This food group also contains vital protein, riboflavin, vitamin A (when fortified), and vitamin D, which helps the body utilize calcium.

BREAKFAST IN A GLASS

For those who have difficulty in eating a nutritious breakfast, the problem may be solved by breakfast in a glass. They can also be used as after-school or between-meal snacks for youngsters. Loaded with protein and vitamins, they are very nutritious and so simple a child can make them. Eggs are the basis for most of them. Use the following recipes as a guide. Although a variety is presented here, I'm sure you'll be able to think up many more. They're great for someone who's ill and doesn't feel like eating.

ORANGE NOG

Has a very pleasing and refreshing flavor.

SINGLE RECIPE
Yield: 1 serving

1 cup reconstituted frozen orange juice
1 egg
2 heaping tablespoons skim dry milk
Dash of superfine sugar or sweetener to taste

DOUBLE RECIPE
Yield: 2 servings

2 cups reconstituted frozen orange juice
2 eggs
4 heaping tablespoons skim dry milk
Dash of superfine sugar or sweetener to taste

Combine all the ingredients in your blender, blend until frothy, and serve immediately.

VARIATION. Add a banana.

CHOCOLATE PEANUT-BUTTER NOG

This unusual combination has the flavor of an "Oh Henry!" bar. It's very nourishing and has great taste appeal, especially with the youngsters.

SINGLE RECIPE
Yield: 1 serving

DOUBLE RECIPE
Yield: 2 servings

1 cup milk
1 egg
¼ cup creamy peanut butter
2 tablespoons instant
  chocolate-flavor mix

2 cups milk
2 eggs
½ cup creamy peanut butter
¼ cup instant chocolate-flavor mix

Combine all the ingredients in your blender and blend until frothy. Serve immediately.

BANANA COFFEE NOG

Yield: 1 serving

1 banana, ¼ cup milk
1 cup milk
1 egg

½ teaspoon vanilla
1 teaspoon instant coffee (optional)

Cut banana into chunks and place in blender, adding ¼ cup milk. Twirl at high speed until banana is liquefied. Add remaining milk, egg, vanilla, and instant coffee and continue beating until mixture is frothy. Pour into a glass and serve immediately.

BROTH NOG

It tastes a bit like lemon-drop soup; because it is nice and hot; it's especially good on cold winter mornings.

Yield: 1 or 2 servings

1 or 2 eggs
1 cup regular strength chicken or beef broth
Parmesan cheese (optional)

Heat the broth (which can be canned, made from bouillon, or homemade) in a microwave oven or on your stove. Meanwhile, twirl the eggs in your blender. With the blender turned on LOW, pour in the boiling broth gradually through the feeder opening. Pour into a large mug or cup. Top with shredded Parmesan cheese if you like.

VARIATION. This same egg nog may be made with 1 cup of hot milk, using 1 teaspoon beef or chicken bouillon granules. This gives it a sort of creamy flavor.

LATIN HOT CHOCOLATE NOG

Yield: 1 serving

1 or 2 eggs	1 tablespoon honey
1 cup hot milk	1 tablespoon instant chocolate-flavor
¼ teaspoon cinnamon	mix

Blend the egg and all ingredients except the hot milk in the blender. Gradually pour the hot milk into the blender, blending all the while. Pour into a large cup or mug and serve immediately.

BREAKFAST HEALTH SHAKE

This has an especially good flavor, tasting somewhat like freshly sliced bananas and cereal. For someone on a low carbohydrate diet, it's ideal.

Yield: 1 serving

1 cup milk	¼ cup wheat germ
½ cup cottage cheese	1 tablespoon honey
1 medium-size banana	

Combine all the ingredients in the blender and purée until just smooth.

VARIATION. Substitute ¾ cup fresh strawberries for the banana; blueberries, raspberries, and other fruits may also be used.

EGGS AND TOAST

YUMMY POACHED EGGS ON TOAST

These eggs, along with milk and juice, make a quick and well balanced breakfast.

1 to 2 tablespoons water	Eggs
½ tablespoon butter	Whole-grain bread, toasted

Heat a large skillet and add water and butter; swirl until butter is melted. Remove from heat, add sufficient eggs for your family (probably no more than 6 eggs will fit in the skillet at one time), cover with a tight-fitting lid, and return to heat. Simmer for about 5 minutes over moderate heat for a soft center, longer if you wish your eggs completely hard. Serve each egg on a buttered slice of toast.

SCRAMBLED EGGS WITH CREAM CHEESE

Scrambled eggs with a different twist. Good to serve all year round.

Yield: 6 servings

6 eggs	Salt and pepper to taste
⅓ cup cream or milk	1 tablespoon butter
1 tablespoon freeze-dried chives	One 3-ounce package cream cheese

Put eggs and cream or milk into blender or mixing bowl. Beat well, add chives, and pour into hot skillet into which butter has been melted. Continue cooking over medium heat, stirring a bit. When eggs begin to set, add slices of cream cheese. Stir briefly and serve immediately while the eggs are still moist and the cheese has just started to melt. Eggs will continue to cook for several minutes after they're removed from burner. Good with hot buttered toast or buns.

BACON TOASTED CHEESE ON RYE

These are always a family favorite and take only a few minutes to prepare. Just as easy to serve one or several.

Thin-sliced rye bread, or any other toasting bread you have on hand
Sharp Cheddar cheese
Bacon (optional)

On a cookie sheet spread as many slices of thin-sliced rye bread as you think your family will eat for breakfast. Place under the broiler, watch closely, and toast on one side. Remove from oven and turn bread, toasted side down. Cover untoasted side with slices of sharp Cheddar cheese and top with precooked bacon strips. Place under the broiler until the cheese is melted and bacon is bubbly, usually just about 2 minutes. Serve immediately.

For small servings use toaster broiler unit. Bacon may also be prepared in microwave oven (see page 43).

OMELETS

Omelets are no more time-consuming or difficult to make than scrambled eggs if you have a properly seasoned skillet. For best results a seasoned omelet pan should not be used for anything else. An 8- or 9-inch skillet is the perfect size for a two- or three-egg omelet. To season pan, heat on low heat for about 7 minutes. Pour a tablespoon or two of oil on skillet and heat until oil starts to sizzle. Pour out excess oil and wipe with paper toweling. A hot skillet may also be rubbed with a small piece of unsalted pork rind until it sizzles; again wipe excess fat with paper toweling. Keep the omelet pan well greased and wipe with a paper towel after each use. *Do not put in dishwasher or wash with detergents.* A two- or three-egg omelet usually serves one or two people, depending on appetite.

PLAIN OMELET

These are absolutely perfect when you're cooking for only one or two.

SINGLE RECIPE
Yield: 1 to 2 servings

2 or 3 eggs	Pinch of salt
1 tablespoon butter	Pinch of pepper (optional)

Heat butter in pan. Beat eggs in bowl with fork or wire whisk, being careful not to overbeat. When butter in pan is hot, add eggs; as edges begin to set, lift up eggs letting uncooked portions run underneath. Shake pan as eggs set to prevent sticking. When set, fold omelet and slip onto serving platter and serve immediately.

CHEESE OMELET. Sprinkle ½ cup grated Cheddar cheese on top of omelet after it has set, just before it is finished cooking. Your cheese will begin to melt before you fold it in half, covering the cheese.

SPANISH OMELET. The sauce can be made ahead of time and kept in the refrigerator. It is a very tasty omelet and one of my favorites. Serve over plain or cheese omelet.

Sauce for Spanish Omelet

Yield: Approximately 1 cup

1 tablespoon oil	6 large olives (green or black), chopped
1 tablespoon butter	
1 heaping tablespoon chopped frozen onions	2 medium size tomatoes, peeled and chopped
1 heaping tablespoon chopped frozen green peppers	¼ teaspoon salt
	Pinch of cayenne

Melt butter and oil in skillet, add onions and green peppers, and sauté a few minutes. Then add olives and tomatoes and cook until moisture has nearly evaporated. Add seasonings.

JELLY OMELET. Spread ¼ to ⅓ cup of your favorite jelly or jam on the omelet before it is finished cooking and before it is folded over. If you have a microwave oven, you may wish to heat about ¼ cup of preserves or jelly, which will make it more liquefied and easier to spread and will also keep your omelet from cooling.

Other ingredients that are marvelous in or on omelets are sautéed mushrooms, onions, and ham slivers.

PANCAKES AND QUICK BREADS

Pancakes and quick breads need not be reserved for weekend breakfasts. Simply gather and combine all the dry ingredients the night before. In the morning just add the liquids (eggs and milk), bake or grill, and serve. Or make a double or triple batch and freeze all "leftovers." Heat your frozen pancakes in the toaster, toaster-broiler, or microwave oven.

PUMPKIN MUFFINS

There are never any leftovers when I serve these. Really delectable.

Yield: Approximately 14 muffins

1½ cups sifted flour	2 eggs
1 cup sugar	½ cup milk
1 teaspoon cinnamon	½ cup pumpkin
½ teaspoon nutmeg	½ cup light seeded raisins
1 teaspoon baking powder	Sugar
¼ cup vegetable oil	

Preheat oven to 350°F. Measure and add all the dry ingredients to your mixing bowl. Add vegetable oil and eggs and mix; then gradually add milk. When mixture is well blended, add pumpkin and mix thoroughly. Add raisins and fill paper-lined muffin tins ¾ full. Sprinkle sugar on top and bake at 350°F for 15 to 18 minutes. Let muffins cool for 5 minutes. Remove from pan and serve with butter or whipped butter and honey (see page 50).

TO FREEZE. Muffins should be completely cooled. Set them on a cooky sheet and freeze. When muffins are frozen, place them in freezer bags, seal, label, date, and return to the freezer.

TO SERVE WHEN FROZEN. Place in a 350°F oven for 5 minutes and serve immediately.

CORNMEAL PANCAKES

Anyone who likes cornbread is sure to like these pancakes.

*Yield: Approximately 36 medium
    size pancakes*

1 cup cornmeal
1 cup flour
½ teaspoon salt
2 eggs

1⅔ cups buttermilk
1 teaspoon baking soda
2 tablespoons melted butter or bacon
    grease

In a large mixing bowl combine cornmeal, flour, and salt. Combine eggs with buttermilk, beating slightly. Dissolve baking soda in buttermilk mixture and add to dry ingredients. Now add melted butter and mix batter until well blended. Pour on heated grill or skillet that has been lightly greased. Use about 2 tablespoons of batter for each pancake, roughly 3 to 3½ inches in diameter. When pancakes are bubbly on top and brown underneath, flip and cook the other side until delicately browned. Serve immediately with honey butter (see below), melted butter, maple syrup, or honey. Good with bacon (see page 43), ham, or sausage.

Honey Butter

Especially great with cornmeal pancakes, cornbread, gingerbread, and waffles, even toast. Make ahead; it keeps well in the refrigerator.

½ cup butter or margarine
½ cup honey

With electric mixer or food processor cream butter until light and fluffy. Slowly add honey. When well combined, refrigerate. Serve at room temperature.

VARIATION. For Cinnamon Honey Butter add ½ to 1 teaspoon cinnamon.

WEEKEND BRUNCHES

GERMAN EGG PANCAKES
(EIER PFANNKUCHEN)

This is a very thin pancake, almost like a crepe. It is 9 inches across and is filled with a variety of fruit, jam, or preserves, rolled up, and then eaten. Really a good meal when served with a variety of fillings, letting each person serve himself or herself.

SINGLE RECIPE
Yield: 10 pancakes

1 cup milk	¾ teaspoon salt
3 eggs	1 tablespoon sugar
1 cup sifted flour	Butter

Combine all the ingredients in your blender and twirl until well blended, or combine half the milk with the eggs, add flour, salt, and sugar at once, and beat with your electric mixer until smooth. Add remaining milk, mixing thoroughly.

In a 9-inch skillet melt 1 teaspoon of butter over moderately high heat. Rotate the skillet so that the butter melts and greases the entire surface. Pour ¼ cup of the batter into the hot skillet, rotating the skillet again so that the batter will spread evenly over the bottom of the pan. Bake only until delicately brown, turning once. Remove from skillet and keep warm until the remaining pancakes are finished.

SERVING SUGGESTIONS. These pancakes taste particularly good when cooked lingonberries are used as a filling. Blueberry and apricot jam, as well as blackberry and elderberry jelly, are other favorite fillings.

SPICY APPLE PANCAKES

For a really different treat try these Spicy Apple Pancakes. Could be served for breakfast, brunch, or dessert. Sure to be a family favorite.

Yield: 6 servings

2 quarts apple slices, fresh or frozen, preferably about ¼-inch to ⅜-inch thick	1 cup milk
	2 eggs
½ cup pancake syrup	1 tablespoon melted or liquid shortening
2 tablespoons butter	½ teaspoon cinnamon
1½ cups biscuit mix	¼ teaspoon nutmeg

Peel, core, and slice apples ¼- to ⅜-inch thick. Combine apples in a skillet with syrup and butter and cook until apples are tender, but still firm (approximately 5 minutes). Meanwhile, combine biscuit mix, milk, eggs, shortening, and spices and mix until batter is smooth. Remove apples from skillet with a slotted spoon and add to pancake batter. Fold very gently so that all the apples are covered. Now lift batter-covered apples onto a lightly greased and hot griddle. Grill until edges are cooked. Turn pancakes once. Serve with remaining syrup (in which apples were cooked) or sour half-and-half and powdered sugar.

BANANA GINGER WAFFLES

Serve these delicious, spicy, fruit-filled waffles for a leisurely weekend brunch. Make a double (or triple) recipe and freeze all leftovers. They make a marvelous work-day treat.

Yield: 4 to 5 servings

2 eggs	¾ teaspoon salt
½ cup brown sugar	1 teaspoon ginger
1 cup buttermilk	1 teaspoon cinnamon
2 ripe bananas, mashed	2 teaspoons baking powder
¼ cup butter or margarine, melted	1½ cups flour

In a medium-sized mixing bowl, combine eggs and sugar, beating until light and fluffy. Add buttermilk, mashed bananas, and melted butter or margarine. Now add seasonings and baking powder. Add flour, mixing until well blended. Pour onto heated waffle grill and bake. Serve with Rum Syrup.

Rum Syrup

½ cup maple or maple flavored syrup
3 tablespoons dark rum (more if desired)

Combine the above ingredients and heat until warm. Serve warm. Some people use more syrup than others, so depending on your preference you may wish to double this recipe. Leftover syrup can be stored in the refrigerator.

OVEN FRENCH TOAST

No standing over a hot griddle or stove with these.

Yield: 8 to 12 slices French Toast

4 eggs	¼ teaspoon nutmeg
1 tablespoon sugar	1½ cups milk
½ teaspoon salt	8 to 12 slices day-old bread

Preheat oven to 475°F. In a shallow dish slightly beat eggs. Add sugar, salt, nutmeg, and milk. Quick work can be made of this step by putting all the ingredients in your blender and then pouring them in the shallow dish. *Generously* butter or grease a large cookie sheet or jelly roll pan. Dip bread into egg and milk mixture, allowing each slice to absorb as much liquid as possible. Place dipped bread on cookie sheet. Bake in preheated 475°F oven for 5 minutes. Turn. Bake about 5 minutes longer or until golden brown. Cut each slice in half. Serve with sausage, jelly, or syrup.

Sandwiches and Light Meals

LUNCHBOX ROUTINE

A lot of time can be saved if you think about the lunch taker when preparing regular meals. Prepare a sufficient quantity of soups, stews, chili, spaghetti, and chop suey so that the lunch takers can have an occasional treat. Leftover meatloaf, sliced and seasoned with chili sauce, makes a marvelous sandwich, as does leftover cold corned beef, roast beef, and lean pork roast spread with horseradish or mustard sauce (see page 91).

Make sandwiches ahead of time and put them in your freezer. Clearly label the type of sandwich. Wrap sandwiches separately in waxed or plastic bags or waxed paper; then place all the sandwiches of one kind in a large container or plastic bag, secure tightly, and label the contents. This allows everyone to take the sandwich of their choice that particular day and assemble their own lunches. Also have fresh fruit, cookies, and celery sticks on hand for them to choose from.

If someone in your family takes a lunch bag or box, here are a few ideas that will help you cope.

A real time-saver is making sandwiches once a week on an assembly line basis. Make several different varieties, enough of each to last a week. Once this system is in operation, your family should have five or more varieties to choose from when packing their lunches. Actually, sandwiches made in this manner and frozen are fresher at noontime than those made in the conventional manner. There is also less chance of harmful bacteria developing.

All breads freeze well. From a nutritional point of view, it is best to use, or at least alternate, whole-grain, enriched white, rye, raisin, egg, oatmeal, Boston Brown, and nut breads. Not only is it more nutritious to serve these breads, but also it adds variety and interest to the lunches. Day-old bread is best for making sandwiches that are to be frozen. Bread can be thawed from the freezer, made into sandwiches, and refrozen. It is one of the few foods that may be refrozen. If your freezer space is very limited, make sandwiches the night before and freeze for added freshness.

Make-ahead Sandwiches

Don't use mayonnaise or salad dressing as a spread.

Don't spread jelly directly onto bread. Rather, cover bread first with a thin layer of soft butter or margarine to avoid jelly soaking into bread.

Don't put carrots, celery, cucumbers, or tomatoes in any of the spreads or fillings that are to be frozen.

Don't use cooked egg whites, as they get rubbery when frozen. Yolks may be poached until firm, then sieved or chopped for egg salad. (Freeze egg whites uncooked and use later for meringue shells, meringue kisses (a cookie), or an angel food cake.

Do spread bread liberally with softened butter, margarine, or cream cheese to keep filling from soaking into bread.

Do use softened cream cheese, plain yogurt, dairy sour cream, and sour half-and-half as a binder when mixing salad-type spreads, such as ham salad and chicken salad.

Do put in olives (black or stuffed), pickles, nuts, water chestnuts, and relishes for celery, cucumbers, and radishes.

Do add lettuce and tomatoes just before sandwiches are to be eaten. (They may be wrapped separately and taken along, then added at lunch time.)

Do slice meat such as beef, chicken, ham, and lunch meat thin. Use several slices per sandwich. Several thin slices are easier to eat, and they seem to taste better.

Do try using nuts, especially chopped peanuts, in sandwiches, i.e., with cream cheese and jelly. Not only are they nutritious, but also they add good texture and taste.

Do use substitutes for mayonnaise and salad dressings, e.g., mustard, ketchup, sour cream, sour half-and-half, yogurt, pickle relish, and cranberry sauce.

Vary your sandwich fillings to avoid monotony.

If you don't have a freezer or you don't like making sandwiches, use the alternate plan called "Everybody Makes His or Her Own Lunch." Be sure to provide all the ingredients in sufficient quantity to last out the week. This way everybody can use their own favorite breads, combined with their favorite fillings, and you avoid comments such as, "That was a dumb lunch you fixed me today," and "You know I don't like jelly with my peanut butter sandwich."

A little supervision will be needed from time to time to see that the lunches are nutritionally balanced. Often the temptation is great to take a bagful of candy or a dozen cookies and forget the sandwich.

Carrot and celery sticks, radishes, and cherry tomatoes may be washed and kept in a plastic bag in the vegetable crisper of your refrigerator. Then each lunch maker can help himself to crispy vegetables. Small salt and pepper shakers are available for lunch takers. These are great to send along with hard-boiled eggs, leftover pieces of fried chicken, tomatoes, radishes, and other fresh vegetables. A variety of fresh fruit in season is a delight.

Small, large-mouth thermal containers are available to pack either hot or cold items for the lunch pail. Items that are to be kept cold can be placed in the cups the night before and refrigerated, or in the case of ice cream, frozen. In the morning the thermal containers are simply removed from the refrigerator or freezer and packed in the lunch box.

Ideas for foods to be placed in thermal containers are puddings and custards, applesauce, stewed fruit, Jello, coleslaw, salads, desserts and ice cream for special treats, and Farmers' Chop Suey (see page 56).

Hot things are best heated and put in thermal containers (that have been warmed with hot water) just before the lunch taker leaves home. Ideas for foods to be taken this way are soups, stews, hot cereals, entrées such as chili, spaghetti and sauce, or chop suey, as well as casserole dishes that have been heated in a microwave oven.

SANDWICH SPREAD

This spread is especially good with cold cuts, corned beef, cold roast beef, and salami.

One 3 ounce package cream cheese	½ teaspoon dry mustard
2 teaspoons horseradish	1 teaspoon finely chopped onion

Have cream cheese at room temperature; cream and add other ingredients. If you like your food rather bland, cut the mustard and horseradish to half the designated amount. This spread keeps well in the refrigerator.

PINEAPPLE HAM SANDWICH FILLING

A delightful and unusual flavor combination.

SINGLE RECIPE
*Yield: Sufficient to generously
fill 6 sandwiches*

One 9-ounce can crushed pineapple,
   well drained
2 tablespoons brown sugar

1½ cups chopped ham
1 tablespoon prepared horseradish

Combine pineapple and brown sugar, stirring well and making sure that all the sugar is dissolved (no lumps). Add ham and horseradish, mixing well. Spread on buttered bread.

VARIATIONS. Finely chopped nuts may be added to this spread for added crunchiness. Mustard may be substituted for the horseradish. Cream cheese or diet cream cheese, called Neufchatel cheese, may be used in place of butter.

FARMERS' CHOP SUEY

Many "brown baggers" are tired of sandwiches, are watching their calories, or are on a low carbohydrate diet. They'll love this. A single recipe makes enough for several days. Not only is it good for you, but also it tastes marvelous!

Yield: About 3½ cups

1 pint large-curd cottage cheese
4 radishes, sliced
2 green onions, snipped, stems and
   all
1 sprig parsley, snipped medium fine

½ cucumber, coarsely chopped
1 medium or small tomato, coarsely
   chopped
Salt and pepper to taste
1 tablespoon plain yogurt

Combine all the above ingredients in a mixing bowl, using a liberal amount of salt and pepper.

A good accompaniment would be a slice of toasted thin-sliced rye bread, which according to its manufacturer has only 30 calories. Pack in large-mouth thermal container.

VARIATIONS. Try seasoned salt, caraway seeds, garlic salt, or a blend of herbs, such as Bon Appetite or Beau Monde. Substitute 1 tablespoon sour half-and-half for the yogurt when you are not watching your weight so closely.

WEEKEND LUNCHES, SUPPERS, OR
LATE EVENING SNACKS

Weekend lunches, suppers, or late night snacks (after an evening of cards or after the theater) are nice times to serve something different. You'll find a variety of recipes in this section that are amazingly simple to prepare. Keep these recipes in mind when unexpected guests drop in. Most of the ingredients are shelf foods that you can always have on hand.

REUBEN SANDWICHES

Named after the restaurant that invented them, these sandwiches have fast become a popular item the nation over. You'll find many variations, and the following is one of the best I have tried. Great for weight watchers, too!

Yield: 5 servings (10 to 12 small sandwiches)

1 loaf thin-sliced rye bread (you'll use about 20 to 24 slices)
Creamy diet margarine
8 ounces sliced Swiss cheese
One 8-ounce can sauerkraut, well drained

½ pound thin-sliced corned beef
Kosher dill pickles
Dijon-style prepared mustard

Remove bread from loaf, two slices at a time. Spread a thin film of creamy margarine on the two outside surfaces. Do this with as many sandwiches as you plan to use. Stack them on a large platter. Now heat your grill. (We use a waffle iron that converts to a grill, but even a skillet may be used.)

While the grill is heating, put the filling in the sandwiches. Cover one unbuttered side with a Swiss cheese slice, then top with a generous amount of sauerkraut. Cover the other unbuttered side of bread with a generous amount of corned beef. Lay this slice on top of the piece of bread with the Swiss cheese and sauerkraut on it and grill until the rye bread is nicely browned on the outside and the cheese has melted on the inside. Serve immediately with sliced kosher pickles and mustard. Open sandwich briefly and insert the pickles and spread the mustard on the corned beef.

VARIATION. You may wish to mix some Thousand Island dressing with the sauerkraut for a creamier flavor. Many restaurants serve it this way; add about 3 tablespoons of dressing to the sauerkraut and mix.

BLUSHING BUNNY

These ingredients can always be on hand for emergency cooking, as when unexpected company arrives or you didn't make it to the grocery store.

Yield: 4 to 5 servings

2 tablespoons butter	1 teaspoon Worcestershire sauce
2 tablespoons flour	1 to 2 packages Holland rusk toast
1 cup milk	rounds
½ pound sharp Cheddar cheese, sliced	Crisp slices of bacon (optional)
	1 15-oz. can tomato sauce
1 tablespoon Dijon mustard (2 tablespoons for additional zip)	with tomato bits or
	1 10¾-oz. can tomato soup

Melt butter in a large skillet and add flour, making a paste. Add milk and tomato sauce with tomato bits or tomato soup. Continue cooking, stirring constantly, until sauce thickens. Add sliced cheese to sauce; lower heat. Continue stirring until cheese melts. Then add mustard and Worcestershire sauce; taste and adjust seasoning.

Spoon sauce on toast rounds and top with bacon, if you wish. Serve immediately. For help-yourself type entertaining, keep the Blushing Bunny sauce in a chafing dish. Have toast rounds and bacon setting on a platter nearby.

VARIATION. For a more substantial meal, place cooked asparagus spears (fresh or frozen) on toast rounds and cover with cheese sauce.

CHEESE FONDUE. The cheese sauce makes a wonderful fondue. Serve with toasted squares or chunks of Italian or French bread.

HOT HAM 'N SWISS ON RYE

That all-time favorite takes on different proportions in this "battered" version. Quick and easy to make.

Yield: 6 sandwiches

12 slices thin-sliced rye bread	1 cup beer
Butter, margarine, or whipped diet margarine	2 eggs
	1 tablespoon paprika
6 slices ham	Mustard
6 slices Swiss cheese	Dill pickles
1 cup flour	

Butter rye bread and fill with ham and cheese. You may add your mustard now or have each person add their own later. Heat your grill and butter lightly. Meanwhile, combine flour, beer, eggs and paprika. (I twirl mine in the blender for just a few seconds and then pour into a shallow pan.) Now dunk each sandwich into this batter and grill until outside is nice and crusty and cheese is bubbly. Serve with mustard and sliced dill pickles.

These sandwiches may also be made with regular rye bread. Calorie watchers will be pleased to know that an ordinary slice of rye bread contains 90 calories, while the thin-sliced rye has only 30. So you can see that, although one of these sandwiches is quite filling, it will be lower in calories than that made with regular rye.

HOT CRABMEAT SANDWICHES

These pretty open-faced sandwiches can be made ahead of time and refrigerated. Just pop into oven before serving.

Yield: 6 servings

½ cup sliced almonds, toasted
One 6-ounce package frozen crabmeat, or one 8-ounce can crabmeat
¼ cup chopped celery
¼ cup mayonnaise or 2 tablespoons mayonnaise and 2 tablespoons yogurt

1 tablespoon lemon juice
3 large English muffins, split, toasted, and buttered
1 ripe avocado, pared and peeled
3 ounces Cheddar cheese, sliced
Paprika
Tomato wedges

Place blanched, slivered almonds on a baking sheet or pie pan and bake at 350°F until nicely browned (about 3-5 minutes) in oven or broiler-toaster.

Thaw frozen crabmeat and drain. Remove any remaining cartilage or shell. Combine almonds, celery, mayonnaise, and lemon juice with crabmeat, tossing lightly. Arrange toasted muffin halves on a cookie sheet, cover with crab mixture, slice avocado, divide evenly, and place on top of the crab mixture. Top with cheese. Sprinkle with paprika and bake in a preheated 400°F oven for about 15 minutes or until topping is heated through and cheese is melted. Serve with tomato wedges.

REUBEN DOGS

Is your family tired of the same old hot dogs? Put some zip into your meals and try these. So easy!

Yield: 6 servings

6 hot dogs
6 hot dog buns
Mustard
One 8-ounce can sauerkraut, well drained

2 tablespoons Thousand Island dressing
¼ pound sliced Swiss cheese
Kosher dill pickle slices or slivers

Heat hot dogs in boiling water, microwave oven, or broiler. Slice hot dogs down the center and place in center of hot dog buns. Spread center of hot dog with a little mustard. Add one-sixth of the sauerkraut topped with 1 teaspoon of Thousand Island dressing. Cover with Swiss cheese and place under the broiler until cheese is melted and bubbly. Garnish with dill pickle slices or slivers and serve immediately.

TASTY CHIPPED BEEF

An old-fashioned treat that can still be enjoyed today. Economical too.

SINGLE RECIPE
Yield: 2 servings

2 tablespoons butter or bacon fat
1½ teaspoons dehydrated minced onion
1½ tablespoons flour
1¼ cups milk
1½ teaspoons instant beef bouillon granules
2 tablespoons commercial sour cream or sour half-and-half
2 tablespoons dry sherry
One 3-ounce package smoked sliced beef or chipped beef
½ of 3-ounce jar sliced mushrooms (optional)
Toast or Holland rusk, baked potatoes, hot baking powder biscuits, or noodles
1 tablespoon snipped parsley
Paprika

DOUBLE RECIPE
Yield: 4 to 6 servings

4 tablespoons butter or bacon fat
1 tablespoon dehydrated minced onion
3 tablespoons flour
2½ cups milk
1 tablespoon beef bouillon granules
¼ cup commercial sour cream or sour half-and-half
¼ cup dry sherry
Two 3-ounce packages smoked sliced beef or chipped beef
One 3-ounce jar sliced mushrooms (optional)
Toast or Holland rusk, baked potatoes, hot baking powder biscuits, or noodles
2 tablespoons snipped parsley
Paprika

Melt butter in large skillet; add minced onions and sauté for 2 minutes. Add flour and stir until completely dissolved. Slowly add milk, stirring constantly. After milk is completely incorporated, add bouillon granules and stir until dissolved. When mixture has thickened and is bubbly, add sour cream and lower heat. Coarsely cut beef with kitchen shears or knife; now add sherry, beef, and mushrooms if desired. (Chipped beef in a jar can also be used. Soak in warm water to remove salt; it may also be necessary to decrease bouillon granules.) Simmer for 5 to 10 minutes. Serve over toast points or rusk, baked potatoes, hot baking powder biscuits, or even noodles. Garnish with parsley and paprika.

Simple Suppers

ONE-POT MEALS

In an effort to save time, some people broil or fry their dinners every evening during their working week. Weekends and holidays are the only times they may vary their menus. Certainly, a broiled steak and tossed salad is one of the quickest and easiest meals possible. This type of cooking can get to be very monotonous; besides, it's also a very expensive way to cook.

The following simple suppers will help get you off the "broil and fry routine." They'll also save you money, as well as time. Many of the recipes can be prepared in larger quantities, so you can freeze the remainder for another time.

These meal-in-one-pot dinners are certainly great for the cook as well as the dishwasher. Most of all, however, they are very convenient for those particular evenings when various members of the family are on conflicting schedules and will be eating at various times. Keep dinner warm on the stove (on simmer), or in your slow cooker, and let each one serve himself or herself whenever it is convenient. (If you have a microwave oven, warming dinners for late-comers is no problem; just fill plate and warm in microwave oven.)

When you make casseroles, soups, or stews, it is wise to prepare a double or triple recipe (depending on the size of your household)—one for the oven today, and the remainder for the freezer, to be served days or weeks later. These may be prepared on weekends when there is more time. Some of the recipes go together quickly and can be cooked either the night before or even in the morning, depending on your particular schedule.

For the one- or two-person household, it is best to follow the recipe as given and then divide into smaller casseroles or baking dishes. That is, a recipe that bakes in a 9 × 13-inch baking dish can easily be divided into two 8-inch deep pie plates or two 9-inch regular pie plates. Making the entire recipe is usually more economical, because you don't have to worry about what to do with half a can of stewed tomatoes and half a can of tomato sauce. Save these recipes for those occasions when guests are expected.

ITALIAN FONDUE

This marvelous dish, when served with a tossed salad, will pinch-hit as a Sunday evening supper. It's great for a late evening snack, as well as for an appetizer. Precooked and sliced sausage can be frozen and kept on hand for last minute cooking. Fresh bread may also be wrapped in foil and frozen (usually in one-third or one-half-pound packages).

Yield: 5 to 6 servings for
supper; 10 to 12 as an
appetizer, less for a snack

1 pound sweet Italian sausage	½ teaspoon oregano
1 pound Cheddar cheese	1 rounded teaspoon fennel
½ pound mozzarella cheese	½ loaf long thin Italian bread

Slit sausage skins with sharp knife and remove. (In some areas sausage can be bought in bulk.) Lay peeled sausages in bottom of skillet; cover with water, bring to a boil, lower heat, and simmer for about 30 minutes. Drain. Thinly slice or grate cheeses and place in skillet (use Teflon-lined or spray with nonstick vegetable coating) over low heat (about 300–325°F). Stir to mix cheese. When all is melted, add drained sausage, which has been sliced or broken up into chunks. Add seasoning and stir.

Slice bread lengthwise down the middle, almost through the bottom crust, but not quite. Now slice across into 1-inch slices to the bottom crust. (This way your loaf will stay intact.) Wrap in foil and heat in a preheated 400°F oven for about 10 minutes just before serving. To keep the bread warm, serve in a bun warmer if you wish.

TO SERVE. Use warmed bread pieces to dunk into cheese and scoop up sausage; this is a finger food and only napkins need be served with it.

VARIATION. For a more zippy flavor use half mild and half sweet Italian sausage. Devotees of hot Italian sausage may want to use only that.

CORNED BEEF DINNER

One of my very favorite meals, because it's so easy to prepare. Leftover meat can be made into such marvelous recipes as Corned Beef Hash, Reuben Sandwiches (see page 57), and just plain corned beef sandwiches with mustard and dill pickle on onion roll.

SINGLE RECIPE
Yield: 6 to 8 servings

One 3- to 4-pound corned beef brisket
Water, to cover
2 large garlic cloves, cut in half
2 bay leaves, crumbled
6 peppercorns

1 medium Spanish onion, sliced, or 6 to 8 small round onions, peeled and left whole
1 head cabbage, cut into wedges and/or 6 to 8 medium size red potatoes, peeled

Cook just sufficient vegetables for one meal (unless, of course, you plan to have the same meal within a few days). If there are four in your family, then use only four wedges of cabbage, four potatoes, and four onions, if you wish. Carrots may also be added or substituted for the onions. Put garlic, bay leaf, and peppercorns in large teaball or wrap in cheesecloth tied with string. If the meal is prepared in a slow cooker, you may wish to cook on low for approximately 10 to 12 hours, or on high for 6 hours (see manufacturer's instructions). This dish can also be prepared in a large dutch oven or similar container on your stove. Place meat in cooking vessel, cover with water, and add seasonings and onions. Bring water to a boil; lower heat; cook for about 4 hours before adding cabbage and potatoes and/or carrots. Continue cooking over low heat for another 2 hours until meat is very tender. Serve with horseradish or mustard sauce (see page 91).

LAZY MAN'S BEEF STEW

This stew can be made in several ways. If you have an automatic timer on your oven, just set the temperature and timer to go on 5 hours before you expect to return home. Add peas upon your return, and 10 minutes later your dinner is ready. Your slow cooker is also perfect for this recipe. It's a great dish to prepare over the weekend in large quantities, serve some, and freeze the remainder for future use.

Yield: 5 to 6 servings

2 pounds lean beef, cut into 1 to 1½-inch cubes

1 envelope (1¼ ounces) beef flavor mushroom soup mix

One 1-pound can stewed tomatoes

6 medium size carrots, pared and sliced into 1-inch pieces

Half a 20-ounce package of frozen small whole onions

1 large Spanish onion, sliced and separated into rings

1 cup frozen peas

Put meat into a large heavy kettle that has a tight-fitting lid. Add soup mix, tomatoes, carrots, and onions. Cover and place in a 275°F oven for about 5 hours. No need to watch this stew or to brown it. Add frozen peas about 10 minutes before serving. Delicious served with dumplings, noodles, or potatoes. Remove meat and vegetables from kettle. Add a little flour that has been thinned with water if the sauce needs to be thickened. This step may or may not be necessary. Pour gravy over meat and vegetables or serve separately as you wish.

VARIATIONS. Peel and add small boiling potatoes along with other vegetables. A 20-ounce package of frozen vegetables for stew may be added as a substitute.

TO FREEZE. Serve your dinner and immediately afterwards put cooled stew into freezing containers. Date, label, seal, and freeze. *Do not* add potatoes to stew that is to be frozen.

 TO SERVE WHEN FROZEN. Partially thaw container of stew. Empty contents into a heavy pan and warm to serving temperature. Do not overcook! Use microwave oven if you have one.

PIZZA CASSEROLE

You may wish to divide this casserole into several small dishes and freeze some for future meals.

Yield: About 2 quarts

8 ounces noodles

1½ pounds lean ground beef

½ cup dairy sour cream or sour half-and-half

One 4½-ounce jar sliced mushrooms (optional)

Three 8-ounce cans pizza sauce

1 tablespoon fennel seeds

1 teaspoon oregano

¼ teaspoon thyme

¼ teaspoon basil

Freshly ground pepper

Salt to taste

One 8-ounce package mozzarella cheese, shredded

Cook noodles in boiling salted water according to package directions. Drain thoroughly. Meanwhile sauté meat in skillet, draining any excess fat. Add sour cream, mushrooms, if desired, pizza sauce, and seasonings. Combine with drained noodles and add half the shredded cheese. Spoon into buttered casserole dish and top with remaining cheese. Bake in a 375°F oven for about 30 minutes.

GROUND BEEF CURRY

This simple meal-in-one-dish has a different and unique flavor. Serve with a tossed salad and dinner is ready.

Yield: 6 servings

1 cup boiling water	1 tablespoon plus 1 teaspoon curry
1 cup dark seedless raisins	1 teaspoon salt
1½ pounds ground beef	⅓ cup chopped pecans
1 cup frozen chopped onions	2 teaspoons bouillon granules
1 cup frozen chopped green peppers	½ cup rice, uncooked
1 tablespoon olive or vegetable oil	

Pour boiling water over raisins. Set aside. In a large heavy skillet brown beef, onions, and green pepper in oil. Pour off any excess drippings, then add curry, mixing well. Now add salt and chopped pecans. Drain raisins, reserving liquid. Add raisins to meat mixture. Add sufficient water to raisin liquid to make 1⅓ cups total. Add to meat along with bouillon granules and rice. Bring to a boil, lower heat, and simmer for 15 minutes. Remove from heat and let steam for another 15 minutes before serving. Add additional water if needed.

VARIATION. If you like a bit more "oomph" to your cooking, add ½ teaspoon (or more, if you're very daring) of hot Madras curry.

BAKED WILD RICE AND BEEF DISH

The combination of wild rice and Swiss cheese gives this casserole a very nutty flavor; however, upon tasting the dish I don't believe you would guess that there was any Swiss cheese in it.

Yield: 6 to 8 servings

One 6-ounce package Uncle Ben's Long Grain and Wild Rice	½ pound Swiss cheese, grated
1 can (10¾ ounces) cream of celery soup, undiluted	1 pound ground beef
	½ cup frozen chopped onions
	Milk

Preheat oven to 300°F. Cook rice according to package directions. Combine cooked rice with cream of celery soup and grated Swiss cheese. Meanwhile, brown ground beef with onions. Then combine with rice mixture in a 9 × 9-inch glass baking dish. Add milk if mixture seems a little dry. Bake in 300°F oven for 45 minutes, or until mixture is nice and bubbly.

TO FREEZE. Freeze unbaked.

TO SERVE WHEN FROZEN. Thaw and follow baking directions above, or put frozen casserole in preheated 300°F oven and bake covered for 1 hour, then uncover. Make sure center of casserole is nice and bubbly. *Do not* bake at higher temperature, as this makes the cheese stringy.

VARIATIONS. This casserole can also be made with chicken. Cook rice in chicken broth and substitute approximately 2 cups of boned chicken for the 1 pound of ground beef. Add ½ cup chopped green pepper to the onions and sauté. Add ¼ cup Parmesan cheese.

HAMBURGER CHOP SUEY

Not authentic—but good.

Yield: 6 servings

1 pound lean ground beef
2 tablespoons vegetable oil
1 bunch green onions, sliced
   diagonally in 1-inch slices
1 green pepper, sliced julienne-style
½ cup celery, sliced diagonally in
   ½-inch slices
One 1-pound can chop suey
   vegetables, drained

One 6-ounce can water chestnuts,
   sliced
1 can (10¾ ounces) condensed
   chicken broth
½ teaspoon garlic salt
½ teaspoon powdered ginger
2 tablespoons soy sauce
1 tablespoon cornstarch
¼ cup sherry

When available, fresh or frozen vegetables, such as pea pods, bean sprouts, etc., may be substituted for canned chop suey vegetables.

Brown beef in oil; add onions, green pepper, celery, and sauté for 5 minutes. Remove any excess drippings. Add chop suey vegetables, water chestnuts, and chicken broth. Now add seasonings and soy sauce. Dissolve cornstarch in sherry, mixing well. Add slowly to hamburger mixture. Continue cooking until mixture thickens and becomes clear. Simmer for 10 minutes. Serve over rice or chow mein noodles.

CHICKEN CHOP SUEY. Substitute 2 cups leftover chicken or turkey, or 2 fresh chicken breasts, for beef. Add ¼ to ½ pound fresh mushrooms or a 4-ounce jar mushrooms.

QUICK HAMBURGER STROGANOFF

When you're pressed for time and still want to serve a pleasing meal, this recipe is a real lifesaver. The Stroganoff can be made at the same time you are boiling your noodles. Toss a salad and your meal is complete.

Yield: 6 servings

One 8-ounce package noodles
1 pound lean ground beef
1–2 tablespoons vegetable oil
1 cup frozen chopped onions
1 cup frozen chopped green peppers

1 package (1⅜ ounces) dry onion
   soup mix
½ to 1 cup milk
1 cup sour half-and-half or sour
   cream

Cook noodles and drain. Meanwhile, sauté beef in vegetable oil. Add frozen onions, green peppers, and onion soup mix. Continue cooking until the onions are clear. Add milk and sour cream. Lower heat and simmer 2 minutes. Arrange cooked noodles on a large serving platter. Pour the Stroganoff mixture over the top, garnish with parsley and paprika, and serve.

TATER TOTS-HAMBURGER CASSEROLE

This quickie has been a lifesaver on many occasions. The ingredients are those you usually have on hand, and they go together quickly! Smaller families can divide the recipe into two deep 8-inch glass pie plates or two shallow 9-inch pie plates and freeze one.

Yield: 10 servings

2¼ pounds lean ground chuck	One 2-pound bag frozen Tater Tots
3 eggs	2 (10¾ ounces) cans cream of
1 cup frozen chopped onions	mushroom soup, undiluted
2 slices bread	1 cup milk
Salt and pepper to taste	2 teaspoons Worcestershire sauce

Preheat oven to 350°F. Combine ground chuck, eggs, onions, bread, salt, and pepper and mix together in your mixing bowl (using your electric mixer if you wish). Pat in the bottom of a 9 × 13-inch baking dish. Place the Tater Tots on top of this, setting them on end. In a separate bowl combine the mushroom soup, milk, and Worcestershire sauce. Pour this mixture over the tater tots and sprinkle with seasoned salt, if desired. Bake at 350°F for 45 minutes to 1 hour.

TO SERVE WHEN FROZEN. Thaw at room temperature or in refrigerator and bake as above, or use your microwave oven.

SKILLET BEEF WITH RICE

An easy, economical dish that can be prepared in minutes.

Yield: Approximately 6 servings

1 pound ground beef	1 can (4 ounces) mushrooms,
⅔ cup chopped frozen onions	drained
⅔ cup chopped frozen green pepper	2 teaspoons salt
3 tablespoons butter	1 cup rice
1 can (1 pound) stewed tomatoes	1 cup sour half-and-half or yogurt
1 can (8 ounces) tomato sauce	

In a large heavy skillet brown beef, onions, and green pepper in butter. Add tomatoes, tomato sauce, mushrooms, and salt. Cook to boiling. Stir in rice and sour half-and-half. Cover and simmer for about 25 minutes, or until rice is tender. Serve.

HAM CASSEROLE

This recipe is so easy, your spouse or children could whip it together in 5 minutes.

Yield: 6 servings

3 cups frozen hashed brown potatoes	¼ teaspoon fresh ground pepper
¾ cup sour cream or sour half-and-half	2 to 3 cups diced cooked ham
2 tablespoons onion soup mix	⅓ cup chopped frozen green peppers, or ⅓ cup sliced stuffed green olives
¾ cup milk	Butter
¾ teaspoon salt	

Mix all the above ingredients and pour into a greased 1½-quart baking dish or casserole. Sprinkle top with bread crumbs and dot with butter. Bake at 350°F for 30 minutes.

FETTUCINE ALLA PAPALINA
(NOODLES WITH EGG SAUCE)

Fettucine Alla Papalina is a first cousin to Noodles Alfredo. A rich egg sauce, together with ham and mushrooms, makes this a marvelous entrée that only requires the addition of crusty Italian or French bread, a vegetable platter, or tossed salad. A marvelous way of using leftover ham.

SINGLE RECIPE	DOUBLE RECIPE
Yield: 2 servings	*Yield: 4 servings*
1 tablespoon butter or margarine	2 tablespoons butter or margarine
1 cup sliced mushrooms	2 cups sliced mushrooms
1 cup julienne strips of cooked ham	2 cups julienne strips of cooked ham
¼ cup chopped frozen onions	½ cup chopped frozen onions
2 egg yolks	4 egg yolks
2 tablespoons grated Parmesan cheese	¼ cup grated Parmesan cheese
3 tablespoons butter or margarine	6 tablespoons butter or margarine
Half an 8-ounce package medium egg noodles, cooked and drained	One 8-ounce package medium egg noodles, cooked and drained
1 tablespoon grated Parmesan cheese	2 tablespoons grated Parmesan cheese
1 tablespoon snipped parsley	2 tablespoons snipped parsley

Sauté mushrooms, ham, and onions in butter or margarine until vegetables and ham are slightly browned. Beat egg yolks in top of a double boiler. Add grated cheese. Cut butter into small slices and stir into egg mixture. Place the egg mixture over hot, not boiling, water. Cook, stirring constantly, until butter melts and the sauce becomes slightly thickened. *Caution:* boiling water will cook eggs too fast, making the sauce lumpy. Pour egg sauce over hot cooked and drained noodles. Toss well to coat the noodles. Add ham and mushroom mixture. Sprinkle with remaining Parmesan cheese and parsley. Toss well and serve immediately.

VARIATION. You may omit the ham or mushrooms and serve the Fettucine as an accompanying dish for chicken, veal, fish, or beef. Always serve it hot and preferably with a fresh, crusty loaf of French or Italian bread.

ORIENTAL DISHES

The following Oriental dishes are perfect for the working person. They need no advance preparation and cook in a hurry. You can buy the ingredients on your way home from work, if necessary, and serve an elegant meal less than a half-hour after you arrive home. Conclude your meal with a blender dessert, and you'll amaze everyone with your quick and efficient cooking routine.

These recipes also give you an excellent opportunity to use a Chinese wok, should you happen to have one. They can, of course, also be prepared in a regular skillet over very high heat.

If fresh pea pods are available, by all means use them instead of frozen pea pods. They have a crispier texture and are also more flavorful. Wash them well and cut off the ends, much as you would with green beans. Sometimes a small string comes off at the same time.

Most of these recipes can easily be divided for the small household. They're a great way to cook for just one or two people.

ORIENTAL BEEF WITH GREENS

This is a real quickie—about 10 minutes to cut and prepare vegetables and about 7 minutes to cook your dinner.

Yield: 6 servings

1¼ pounds sandwich steak, cut into ¼-inch strips
1½ pounds celery cabbage (about half of a large stalk)
3 green scallions, tops and all
Toasted sesame oil, peanut oil, or salad oil

2 teaspoons soy sauce
½ teaspoon salt
1 cup chicken broth (canned is fine)
1 tablespoon cornstarch
1 tablespoon water

Stack trimmed sandwich steaks one on top of the other and slice into ¼-inch strips. Set aside. Wash celery cabbage, pull off the outer leaves, wash them well in cold water, and drain on absorbent toweling. Slice scallions into ½-inch diagonal slices. Slice celery cabbage in the same manner.

Heat skillet with 2 tablespoons of peanut or vegetable oil until smoking. Add meat and continue stirring, cooking rapidly until color is gone. Remove meat from skillet. Add additional oil to skillet. When oil is very hot add celery cabbage and scallions, cooking about 3 minutes until crispy tender.

Now add cooked beef, soy sauce, salt and chicken broth. Blend cornstarch with water and add to broth, stirring until mixture thickens. Adjust seasonings and serve immediately over hot rice.

ORIENTAL SHRIMP DE JONGHE

Don't let this long list of ingredients fool you; it's quick and easy to prepare. Make in one large or six individual portions. Can be made ahead and then just heated at serving time.

Yield: 6 servings

1 cup uncooked rice	½ teaspoon ginger
4 green onions, snipped	1 teaspoon salt
3 cloves garlic, pressed	Freshly ground pepper to taste
¼ cup butter	½ cup sherry
1 cup water	2 tablespoons soy sauce
¼ cup finely chopped parsley	1½ pounds raw, shelled, deveined
½ teaspoon chervil	shrimp
1 teaspoon tarragon vinegar	½ cup dry bread crumbs
¼ teaspoon thyme	2 tablespoons butter, melted

Sauté rice along with onions and garlic in butter over moderate heat until brown. (Do not use instant rice.) Add water, chopped parsley, chervil, vinegar, thyme, ginger, salt, and pepper. Lower heat, cover, and cook rice according to directions on package.

After rice is completely cooked, add sherry and soy sauce. Place rice mixture in alternate layers with shrimp in individual ramekins or sea shells or in a 1½-quart casserole dish. Combine melted butter with bread crumbs; sprinkle on top and bake in a preheated 350°F oven for 1 hour (for a large casserole dish), or until nicely browned. Forty-five minutes usually is sufficient for the individual ramekins or sea shells. Test frequently to make sure the mixture is not overcooked or the shrimp will toughen.

SHRIMP WITH PEA PODS

Very little advance preparation needed. Cooking time is less than 10 minutes.

Yield: 4 servings

1 pound fresh pea pods, or two
6-ounce packages frozen pea pods, thawed
One 6-ounce can water chestnuts, sliced
One 1-pound bag frozen cleaned and deveined shrimp, thawed
2 teaspoons cornstarch dissolved in ⅓ cup soy sauce

4 tablespoons peanut or salad oil
1 large clove garlic, minced
½ teaspoon ginger
1 teaspoon instant chicken bouillon granules dissolved in ¼ cup hot water
¼ teaspoon sugar
Salt and pepper to taste

When you use fresh pea pods, wash and trim off ends. Dry thoroughly on paper toweling. Slice water chestnuts into ¼-inch slices. Thaw shrimp and drain thoroughly on paper toweling. Dissolve cornstarch in soy sauce. Have other seasonings on hand. This dish is cooked very rapidly at very high heat, so all the ingredients should be conveniently at hand. If you are going to serve this with rice, have your rice cooked before you start cooking your shrimp mixture.

In a large wok or skillet heat oil until smoking. Add pea pods and stir rapidly for about 2 minutes. Remove from heat and remove pea pods from pan. Add more oil if necessary. Add garlic and ginger to oil, then add shrimp. Continue cooking over high heat until shrimp are pink and firm, about 3 minutes. Do not overcook. Add pea pods, water chestnuts, cornstarch mixture, chicken bouillon granules, and remaining seasonings. Cook, stirring rapidly, for 1 more minute. Serve immediately.

STIR-FRIED CHICKEN WITH PEA PODS

The ginger gives this dish a bit of zing!

Yield: 6 servings

2 large whole chicken breasts (about ¾ pound each), deboned and skinned
¼ cup cornstarch
1 egg white
2 tablespoons rice wine or pale dry sherry
¼ pound fresh mushrooms, sliced
½ pound fresh snow peas, or One 6-ounce package frozen pea pods, thawed

4 tablespoons peanut or vegetable oil
½ teaspoon salt
2 slices fresh ginger root, about 1 inch in diameter, or ¼ teaspoon powdered ginger
One 6-ounce can water chestnuts, sliced
½ cup cashew nuts
Salt and pepper to taste

If possible, have your butcher debone the chicken breasts for you. If this isn't possible, cut the chicken breasts in half and run your thumbnail under the breast bone, gently pulling it loose and separating the bone from the breast. Skin by gently pulling skin from breast, separating with a knife where necessary. Lay chicken breasts flat on cutting board and cut into paper thin slices. Then cut crosswise so that each slice is about 2 inches long. Dust chicken pieces in cornstarch. Combine egg white with wine in blender and set aside.

Have mushrooms sliced. If pea pods are fresh, they should have their ends trimmed. While frozen pea pods may be substituted, they will not be as crispy and crunchy as the fresh pea pods. Have all the ingredients assembled. Just before serving, heat wok or skillet over high heat. When properly heated, add 1 tablespoon of oil and heat for another few seconds until the oil begins to smoke. Add mushrooms, snow peas, and ½ teaspoon of salt. Stir-fry over moderately high heat for 2 minutes. (If using a wok, stir with a wooden spoon in a circular motion, dipping the vegetables in and out of the oil at the side of the pan.) After 2 minutes, remove vegetables from skillet, add remaining 3 tablespoons of oil, again heating until oil almost smokes. Drop in ginger slices or powdered ginger and continue cooking for about 30 seconds. Remove ginger slices. Meanwhile, pour wine–egg white mixture over the chicken pieces and toss until all the chicken is coated. Add to hot skillet and stir-fry for about 2 minutes or until pieces are firm and white. Then add cooked vegetables, sliced water chestnuts, and cashew nuts. Heat for another few minutes until everything is piping hot and ingredients are coated with a clear glaze. If more liquid is needed, add more wine. Salt and pepper to taste. Transfer to a heated platter and serve at once with steaming hot rice.

Soups

Soups are a marvelous way of getting a good amount of vital nutrition on the table in a wholesome and acceptable manner. When soups are properly prepared (this does not have to be a time-consuming job), even the most recalcitrant diner will succumb. The availability of good canned chicken and beef broth often eliminates hours of stove-top cooking. With the aid of canned broth, a blender, and other modern conveniences, homemade soups can be made with little or no effort and yet have the same taste as those that were carefully simmered and watched over for days.

Served with crusty French or Italian bread, breadsticks, crackers, or freshly baked refrigerator biscuits, as well as a mouth-watering dessert, homemade soup makes a very filling, inexpensive, nourishing, and satisfying meal. Leftover soup makes an ideal weekend lunch or light supper. It is also a welcome change from sandwiches for the "brown bagger." Heat and pour into a wide-mouth thermos. With crackers and fruit, what more could anyone want?

Light, clear, or creamy soups are a delightful first course for any meal, but particularly when you are entertaining. They are also a wonderful way to stretch a simple or leftover meal.

Soups can be great time- and money-savers. They can be an energy-saver as well if you use your slow cooker (see page 34). Slow cookers make marvelous stockpots and soup pots; they are absolutely perfect for the busy person. Because they are thermostatically controlled, these slow cookers can simmer night and day without a worry about scorching pots or cooking dry.

When sour cream has been added to a broth, soup, or sauce, be careful to keep it under the boiling point. Otherwise, it may curdle and separate.

Seasonings

Quite frequently a Bouquet Garni is needed for seasoning. Use a very large teaball with a chain and hook. Into this put a dozen peppercorns, a bay leaf, parsley, and a few pinches of basil and marjoram. I suggest the large teaball so that the seasonings can be removed at the end of cooking without the need for straining. It is a real time-saver and much easier than the recommended cheesecloth. Use bouillon granules instead of salt for flavor. Taste after each addition, so you don't end up with a salty soup. Onion, garlic, and celery salt are another interesting way to add flavor to your broth.

For a more full-flavored soup learn to salt with bouillon cubes and chicken or beef extract. Both have a very high salt content. Most canned beef broth has a very peculiar flavor, so unless you can purchase a brand that really tastes like beef broth, you are better off using water and flavoring it with beef extract and bouillon granules.

Defatting and Clarifying Stock

The easiest way to remove all fat from your broth or soup is simply to refrigerate it. The fat will harden on top of the liquid and can easily be removed. This takes extra time and planning ahead, and is not always possible. A heavy layer of fat can be removed with a baster or gravy ladle. Skim top liquid carefully and pour it into a large measuring cup and place in your freezer or refrigerator until the fat solidifies. Adding a few ice cubes should hasten this process. Remove solidified fat and return the remaining broth to stock.

If scum appears on top of stock, skim immediately. You may be cooking stock at too high a temperature. To clarify broth, strain through a very fine sieve or wet muslin. The sieve is easiest to use; these especially fine sieves can be found in specialty stores, as well as the housewares section of the larger department stores. It is a must if you plan on making stock often.

Using Leftovers

Soups are a convenient way of using leftovers. Use leftover fish and seafood in chowder; ham cubes in split-pea or green pea soup, as well as lentil, potato, or minestrone soup. Leftover roast beef, chicken, and pot roast are great in beef vegetable, minestrone, and other beef broth soups. Use leftover peas and carrots in beef vegetable or minestrone soups, as well as dabs of rice, macaroni, and other small pastas. Leftover potatoes also go well in soups. Cut them in cubes and make Quick Potato and Bacon Soup (see page 77), Hearty Ground Beef Soup, or Meatball Soup. Accompany with salad and crusty bread, crackers, breadsticks, dumplings, or rolls.

MEATBALL SOUP

Packed with vitamins, low in calories, inexpensive, and yet extremely tasty and easy to prepare. What more could any cook ask for?

Yield: Approximately 3 quarts

1½ pounds lean ground beef
1½ teaspoons seasoned salt
¼ teaspoon freshly ground pepper
2 eggs
¼ cup chopped parsley
⅓ cup cracked wheat or wheat germ
1 large can (1 quart 14 ounces)
   vegetable juice cocktail
3 tablespoons barley
1 tablespoon instant bouillon
   granules

1 medium size onion, thinly sliced
2 medium size carrots, thinly sliced
3 ribs celery, diced
1½ cups frozen kernel corn, or one
   12-ounce can kernel corn
2 cups frozen hashed brown
   potatoes
2 bay leaves
1 tablespoon sugar
Salt and pepper to taste

With your mixer combine the ground beef, seasonings, eggs, parsley, and wheat germ. Beat until well blended and fluffy; form into balls about 1 inch in diameter.

Meanwhile, in a large kettle bring the vegetable juice cocktail to a boil. Add barley and bouillon granules. Drop meatballs into this mixture and simmer for about 15 minutes. Now add vegetables, remaining seasonings, and continue cooking over low heat until the vegetables are crispy tender (about 30 minutes). Serve immediately.

If this makes too large a quantity for your family, immediately freeze that portion which you will not be using. Store in freezer containers for several months.

HEARTY GROUND BEEF SOUP

I always have the ingredients on hand for this delicious soup. It is a great standby when time is short or the cupboards are bare.

Yield: About 4 quarts

1½ to 2 pounds lean ground beef
1 to 2 tablespoons cooking oil
1 tablespoon instant beef bouillon
   granules
½ teaspoon pepper
Salt to taste
½ teaspoon garlic powder
½ teaspoon basil
2 cans (10 ¾ ounces) chicken broth

1 can (10 ¾ ounces) beef bouillon
1 cup frozen chopped onions
¼ cup raw rice
One 20-ounce package frozen mixed
   vegetables
One 1-pound can stewed seasoned
   tomatoes
One 15-ounce can tomato sauce with
   tomato bits

Brown beef in large dutch oven or skillet, using as little cooking oil as possible. Drain off excess fat. Add seasonings and broth, together with an equal amount of water. Add onions and rice and bring mixture to a boil. Cover, lower heat, and simmer gently for 1 hour. Add frozen vegetables, tomatoes, and tomato sauce. Bring to a boil, then lower heat and simmer for 10 minutes. Serve.

If you are in a hurry, start cooking broth and rice in a separate kettle. While it is heating you can brown meat and sauté onions.

I particularly like the mixed vegetables with okra in it, even though okra is not one of my favorite vegetables. It adds a certain texture and flavor to the soup. You may wish to vary this according to your own taste.

BEAN SOUP

For a marvelous, economical meal-in-one dish, try this Bean Soup with ham. Serve with crusty French bread and butter, and your meal is complete.

Yield: Approximately 4 quarts

One 16-ounce package navy beans
   (approximately 2 cups)
3 quarts water
1 center cut ham slice
   (approximately 1½ to 2 pounds),
   coarsely cubed
1 cup celery, coarsely cut
1 cup carrots, coarsely cut
1 cup chopped frozen onions

1 bay leaf
2 large cloves garlic, minced
2 tablespoons flour
1 tablespoon brown sugar
One 16-ounce can seasoned stewed
   tomatoes
Approximately 4 tablespoons instant
   bouillon granules (less if ham is
   salty)

The night before, pick over and wash beans, cover with cold water, and soak overnight. In the morning drain beans, place them in a very large kettle, and add the 3 quarts of water, less 1 cup, and the coarsely cubed ham. With the reserved 1 cup of water combine celery, carrots, and onions in your blender or food processor. Chop coarsely and add to bean mixture. Add bay leaf and garlic. Bring to a boil and simmer for several hours.

One hour before serving, combine the 2 tablespoons of flour with some of the broth and the brown sugar, mixing well. When mixture is blended, add to soup, stirring until dissolved and soup is thickened. Add stewed tomatoes and bouillon granules, tasting as you go until the right amount of salt and flavoring has been added. Serve at once.

LENTIL SOUP

A good way to use leftover ham and ham bones. Particularly good on a cold winter evening.

Yield: 2 quarts

1-pound bag lentils	Several sprigs of parsley
6 cups water (add additional water as needed)	1 medium size onion
	1 potato
Ham bone (optional)	1 bay leaf
1-pound ham, cut coarsely (optional)	Freshly ground pepper
2 carrots	2 tablespoons plus 1 teaspoon
3 ribs of celery	instant bouillon granules.

Wash lentils with cold water and put into soup kettle. Add 5 cups of water, ham bone, and ham. In your blender or food processor combine remaining 1 cup water, carrots, celery ribs, parsley, onion, and potato. Whirl until finely grated. Add to soup mixture, along with bay leaf, ground pepper, and half of bouillon granules. Bring mixture to a boil, lower heat, and simmer for several hours. Taste your soup. If it needs more salt, add additional bouillon granules, making certain that the soup will not be too salty. Use fewer bouillon granules if ham is salty or ham bone is giving salty flavor to broth. Remove bay leaf.

Serve with a cruet of wine vinegar and let each person season their own soup. Any leftover soup may easily be frozen for future meals.

QUICK POTATO AND BACON SOUP

This soup can be made at a minute's notice. It's very nourishing, with a full-bodied flavor.

Yield: 6 servings

6 medium size red potatoes	1 tablespoon beef stock
1 cup boiling water	1 tablespoon plus 1 teaspoon instant chicken bouillon granules
1 cup milk	
1 cup commercial sour cream or sour half-and-half	6 slices bacon, or ⅓ cup crispy crumbled bacon
Pepper to taste (be generous)	Chopped chives

Peel and cut potatoes into ¼-inch slices. Add water and cook, covered, over moderately high heat until potatoes are tender. While the potatoes are cooking, assemble all the other ingredients, except chives and bacon, and put into the blender. Drain potatoes and measure liquid; add enough milk to make 1 cup. Add cooked potatoes with liquid to ingredients in blender and turn blender on high speed for 30 seconds. Return to pan. Heat and add bacon bits. Garnish each bowl with scissor-snipped chives, and serve.

CREAM OF ONION SOUP

This delicious creamy soup takes only minutes to prepare because it's all put together in your blender or food processor.

Yield: Approximately 2½ quarts

3 large sweet Spanish onions,
  coarsely sliced
2 (10 ¾ ounces) cans chicken broth,
  undiluted
½ cup water
1½ tablespoons butter
2 medium size potatoes, peeled and
  coarsely sliced

1 cup whipping cream
1 cup milk
1½ teaspoons salt
¼ teaspoon white pepper
chopped parsley, cooked and
  crumbled bacon, chives, or
  croutons for garnishes

Cook onion slices in broth and water with butter for 20 minutes. Add potatoes and cook an additional 15 minutes, or until potatoes are tender. Purée in blender, adding cream, milk, and seasonings. Return mixture to stove, bring to a boil, lower heat, and simmer for about 10 to 15 minutes. Adjust seasoning and add garnishes. Serve immediately.

HOT CABBAGE SOUP (KAPUSTA)

This ethnic soup, which is Jewish in origin, is very tasty and hearty, and has a delightful sweet-sour flavor.

Yield: 2½ quarts

One 2-pound head cabbage,
  shredded (about 10 cups)
3 tablespoons kosher salt
½ teaspoon white pepper
1 cup frozen chopped onions
1½ pounds lean beef chuck, cut into
  1-inch cubes
1 large soup bone (about 2½ pounds)

Two 16-ounce cans tomato purée
Two 16-ounce cans stewed tomatoes
1 large potato, pared and cubed (1½
  cups)
1 teaspoon sour salt
1 cup sugar
2 cloves garlic, minced

In a large 6-quart kettle combine cabbage, kosher salt, pepper, onions, and 1½ quarts water. Cover and bring to a boil. Add beef, soup bone, tomato purée, and stewed tomatoes. Bring to a boil again, reduce heat, and simmer covered for 1 hour. Add potatoes and simmer for an additional hour. Twenty minutes before serving time, add sour salt and sugar. Five minutes before serving, add garlic. Remove soup bone. Pour into soup tureen or individual bowls and serve.

MEXICAN LIME SOUP

This very refreshing lime soup is delicious served on a hot day.

Yield: 6 servings

2 cups boned chicken	½ teaspoon coriander
5 cups chicken stock	1½ teaspoons salt
½ cup fresh lemon juice	1 teaspoon oregano
2 tablespoons fresh lime juice	Black pepper to taste
½ cup fresh orange juice	4 drops Tabasco sauce
1 medium size onion, cut into wedges	5 tortillas
1 large green pepper, cut into 1-inch squares	One 1-pound can stewed tomatoes
	1 lime, sliced thin

Boned chicken may be fresh or cooked. If uncooked, simmer for 15 minutes in chicken stock to which lemon, lime, and orange juices, onion, green pepper, and spices have been added. Meanwhile, prepare tortillas by cutting them in half and then into ½-inch strips. Fry in vegetable oil until crispy and drain on paper toweling. Remove chicken from broth, cut into bite-size pieces (if necessary), and return to stock. Add tomatoes and sliced lime. Simmer for an additional 10 minutes.

TO SERVE. Place a portion of fried tortillas in each soup bowl and add soup, making sure that each serving receives a slice of lime as a garnish.

GREEN VEGETABLE SOUP

This soup has practically no calories in it. It is one of the most delightful and delicious soups that I have come upon in a long time. When eating something like this, I always wonder how anything so delicious could be so good for you.

Yield: Approximately 2 quarts

4 cups chicken or beef broth, unsalted (not canned)
1 bunch watercress
½ head iceberg lettuce
4 scallions and tops
Fresh green tops of 1 bunch celery
¼ of a small head of cabbage

½ bunch parsley with stems removed
1 teaspoon thyme
1 tablespoon plus 1 teaspoon instant beef bouillon granules
1 cup sour half-and-half or yogurt
Pepper to taste

This soup can be made in two ways. All the vegetables may be chopped fine with the metal blade of a food processor and added to the broth, or they may be put in whole, simmered for about 30 minutes, and then twirled in a blender. The flavor, if not the texture, is the same. I always used the blender method before I had a food processor; however, I do think that the texture of the finely chopped vegetables is very desirable. Add the sour half-and-half either into the blender or at the end of the cooking period. Adjust the seasoning and serve at once.

VARIATIONS. A nice addition to this soup would be garlic-seasoned croutons or crisp bacon bits sprinkled on top.

VEGETABLE MEDLEY IN BEEF BROTH

A marvelous recipe to have when you just have dibs and dabs of vegetables on hand.

Yield: 6 to 8 servings

One 10¾-ounce can condensed beef broth
One 1-pound can stewed tomatoes
1 large green pepper, cut into 1-inch squares
1 cup diagonally sliced celery
1 cup sliced carrots
1 cup large shell macaroni

1 Spanish onion, sliced
Salt and freshly ground pepper to taste
⅛ teaspoon garlic powder
1 tablespoon cornstarch
1 tablespoon water
¼ cup (approximately) Parmesan cheese

Combine all the ingredients with the exception of the cornstarch, water, and Parmesan cheese in a large kettle. Bring to a boil, lower heat, and simmer until macaroni and vegetables are crispy tender. Dissolve cornstarch in water and add. Continue cooking until soup is clear. (The cornstarch will only thicken broth slightly.) Serve in individual bowls. Sprinkle with Parmesan cheese.

PEANUT BUTTER SOUP

This is a popular recipe in certain sections of the South, but it is not well known in most of our country. It has a very pleasant and unique flavor and is very simple to prepare. Try it as a first course and surprise your family or friends. Don't tell them the ingredients; have them guess.

Yield: Six ½-cup servings

3 tablespoons butter
¾ cup frozen chopped onions
2 ribs celery, finely diced
3 tablespoons flour
3 cups chicken broth, heated
2 or 3 teaspoons instant bouillon
  granules (to taste)

½ cup peanut butter, crunchy or
  smooth
Dash celery salt
1 tablespoon lemon juice
Chopped parsley

Melt butter in a saucepan, add onions and celery, and sauté for about 5 minutes. (Do not brown.) Add flour and mix until well blended. Add warm chicken broth and bouillon granules and simmer for 30 minutes. Blend vegetable mixture in blender for 1 minute. Add peanut butter, salt, and lemon juice and continue blending until well mixed. Pour back into saucepan and simmer until serving time. Top with chopped parsley.

CREAM OF PARSLEY SOUP

If you use canned chicken broth, this soup is a real quickie to make. Serve as a first course or for a light supper or lunch.

Yield: Approximately 5 cups

Two 10¾-ounce cans chicken broth
1⅓ cups water
2 teaspoons instant beef bouillon
  granules
2 cups coarsely snipped parsley
2 egg yolks

1 pint sour half-and-half or yogurt
2 tablespoons lemon juice
¼ teaspoon white pepper (or more
  to taste)
Croutons
Parsley sprigs

Simmer chicken broth with water, bouillon granules, and parsley for 20 minutes. Put egg yolks and sour half-and-half in blender and mix for 1 minute. Add warm broth gradually to the egg-cream mixture. Continue blending at low speed until all the broth has been added. Cover securely and blend at high speed until parsley is finely chopped. Return to saucepan; add lemon juice and pepper. Top with croutons and fresh sprigs of parsley.

EGG DROP SOUP

One of the easiest soups ever. Great for calorie watchers! Goes especially well as a first course with any Oriental entrée. (See pages 69–72).

SINGLE RECIPE
Yield: 4 servings

3 cups rich chicken stock, fresh or canned
1 tablespoon beef bouillon granules
1 tablespoon cornstarch
3 tablespoons chicken stock or cold water

1 tablespoon toasted sesame oil
2 eggs, slightly beaten
Salt and pepper to taste
2 scallions, snipped finely

Heat chicken stock in a saucepan and bring to a boil. Add bouillon granules. Dissolve cornstarch in cold chicken stock or water. When blended, pour into hot chicken stock, continue stirring over moderately high heat until mixture becomes slightly thicker and clearer. Add sesame oil, again stirring slightly. (Toasted sesame oil can be found in the Oriental section of your supermarket. Do not confuse it with regular sesame oil from the near East, which is used as a cooking oil and does not have the full-bodied nutty flavor of toasted sesame oil.) Pour eggs slowly into chicken stock just before serving, stirring it gently once or twice with a spoon. Remove from heat immediately. Adjust seasoning. A ¼ teaspoon of white pepper will give your soup some zip. Garnish soup with chopped scallions.

Meat, Fowl, and Fish

When preparing a new recipe, always remember that it will take longer to prepare the first time you try it. You will be spending more time reading and rereading the recipe. After having tried a new recipe, always make notations, right in your cookbooks. Notations should include information as to how well you liked it, how easy you thought it was, and what changes you would like to make the next time you try the recipe. Just as no two cooks prepare anything exactly the same, no two people usually agree on the exact seasonings to use. Some like their food more spicy or salty than others, so adjust the recipe according to your own taste and preferences.

Here are some helpful hints for the small household. If you are cooking for one, two, or three, you will have to learn how to divide recipes in half or in thirds, or prepare a regular recipe in smaller dishes. Have a variety of small casseroles on hand; the kind that can go from freezer to oven to table. Unfortunately, space does not permit me to give specific recipe information for every size family (see page 14 for dividing recipes). With a little practice you'll quickly get the hang of it. When you divide recipes remember this: a recipe that ordinarily requires a 9 × 13-inch pan will make up into two deep-dish 8-inch pie plates or two 9-inch normal pie plates. A recipe stating that yields 1½ quarts can easily be divided into three pint-size casserole dishes. Be sure to add notations to your recipes as you're cooking, so that you will know the exact size casserole or dish to use the next time you prepare the recipe.

Things Your Mother May Never Have Told You

When browning meat chunks or pieces, don't overload your skillet. Meat should be in a single layer without touching. Otherwise, you will be stewing the meat in its own juice, rather than browning it. Use a very large skillet and do it in several batches, if necessary.

Never carve meat or poultry immediately after removing it from the oven. For a small roast or bird (3 to 5 pounds) allow 10 minutes. For a large roast or turkey (15 pounds or more) wait at least 20 minutes before carving.

If a sauce or gravy becomes lumpy or curdled, pour it all into your blender and mix at high speed. It will become as smooth as velvet.

BEEF

BEEF-NOODLE CASSEROLE ALMONDINE

This is one of those versatile dishes that is the perfect thing to serve for a buffet or potluck dinner. Divided into smaller casseroles it makes a great entrée for a family meal. Every cook should have a few recipes like this in her collection.

Yield: 10 to 12 servings

1 8-ounce package egg noodles
1 can condensed cream of
  mushroom soup (10¾ ounces)
1 cup slivered almonds, toasted
1 cup cottage cheese
1 cup sour cream or sour
  half-and-half
¼ cup finely snipped parsley
3 green onions, sliced finely, tops
  and all
½ teaspoon garlic powder

1 teaspoon oregano, crushed
1 teaspoon salt
Pepper to taste
2 pounds ground beef, lean
1 tablespoon vegetable oil
Additional butter if needed
½ pound fresh mushrooms, sliced
1 cup fine bread crumbs or ½ cup
  crumbs and ½ cup wheat germ
3 tablespoons butter, melted

Cook noodles according to package directions. Drain when *al dente;* it's best to undercook any pasta that is to be added to a casserole. In a large mixing bowl combine the cream of mushroom soup, slivered almonds, cottage cheese, sour cream, parsley, onions, and seasonings. Meanwhile, in a large skillet brown the meat in oil. Remove meat, add more butter if necessary, and sauté mushrooms. Combine meat and mushrooms with cheese sauce and drained noodles. Toss well but gently and arrange in a 9 × 13-inch buttered casserole dish. You can divide it into smaller casseroles, if desired, and freeze it before baking. Combine butter with bread crumbs, sprinkle over the top, and bake in a 350°F oven for 25 minutes.

HAWAIIAN MEATBALLS

These are especially tasty, with a real authentic Polynesian flavor. Make a double batch and freeze the remainder. You'll be glad you did. Brown meatballs in oven for speedy preparation.

Yield: 6 to 8 servings

2 slices bread (white, cracked, or whole wheat)
¼ cup milk
1 egg
2 pounds lean ground beef
2 tablespoons dehydrated minced onions
2 cloves garlic, crushed
1 teaspoon salt
¼ teaspoon white pepper
2 tablespoons vegetable oil
2 ribs celery, sliced diagonally
1 large green pepper, cut into squares

4 green onions, sliced into ¼-inch pieces
One 5-ounce can Chinese water chestnuts, sliced
One 14-ounce can pineapple tidbits, unsweetened
One 10¾-ounce can chicken broth
½ cup cider vinegar
⅓ cup brown sugar, firmly packed
½ teaspoon ground ginger
3 tablespoons cornstarch
⅓ cup soy sauce
3 cups cooked long grain white rice

In a large mixing bowl pour milk over bread and let set for a few minutes. Add egg, ground beef, onions, garlic, and seasonings. Mix with your electric mixer or by hand until evenly blended. Shape into 2-inch balls.

To save time when browning meatballs, instead of using a skillet on top of the stove, you may wish to arrange the meatballs on the rack of your broiling pan and bake them in a 350°F oven for 10 to 20 minutes (until nicely browned). Put about ¼ inch of water in the bottom of your broiling pan so the drippings won't burn. Repeat until all the meatballs are browned. With this method you will not need the 2 tablespoons of vegetable oil, which will also reduce the caloric content of your finished product. After all the meatballs have been browned, set aside and keep warm. Sauté vegetables in drippings, adding a little bit of chicken broth as necessary. Stir to dissolve all the drippings. When vegetables have cooked about 3 minutes and are just crispy tender, add pineapple, remaining chicken broth, vinegar, brown sugar, and ginger.

Dissolve cornstarch in soy sauce, adding 1 tablespoon of water, if necessary. Pour slowly into vegetable mixture and continue stirring as mixture thickens and comes to a boil. Return meatballs to sauce, reduce heat, and simmer for 15 to 20 minutes. Serve over freshly cooked rice.

TO FREEZE. Freeze in broth with vegetables in tightly covered container or heat-and-seal pouches. Don't forget to label and date. Heat-and-seal pouches are very convenient, especially for individual or small portions.

TO SERVE WHEN FROZEN. Thaw in refrigerator or microwave oven. Heat slowly on stove top or in microwave oven.

JIFFY LASAGNE

A quick and easy casserole dish that incorporates all the good old-fashioned flavor of the genuine lasagne; however, this one is made using many shortcuts. It can easily be divided into individual portions.

Yield: Approximately 4 quarts

1 package (1½ ounces) spaghetti sauce mix
One 6-ounce can tomato paste
2 pounds lean ground beef, or half beef and half Italian sweet sausage
1½ teaspoons salt
¼ teaspoon pepper
One 6- or 7-ounce package macaroni

One 8-ounce can pizza sauce
1 pound ricotta or dry cottage cheese
1 pound mozzarella cheese, shredded
½ cup grated Parmesan or Romano cheese
¼ cup snipped parsley

Prepare spaghetti sauce according to package directions, using *tomato paste*. Meanwhile, brown beef; add prepared sauce, salt, and pepper. Simmer for about 20 minutes. Cook macaroni according to package directions. Drain and rinse with hot water. Combine macaroni, pizza sauce, ricotta cheese, and mozzarella cheese in a very large pan or bowl and add meat sauce. Spread meat and sauce mixture into a large 9 × 13 × 2-inch baking dish or several smaller casserole dishes sufficiently large to serve your family for one meal. Mix Parmesan cheese with parsley and spread over meat mixture. Bake in a 325°F oven for 30 minutes or until bubbly. Let stand about 5 or 10 minutes before serving.

CRUNCHY MEATLOAF

The sesame seeds, green pepper, and chopped onions give this meatloaf a nice texture. The leftovers are particularly good sliced cold.

SINGLE RECIPE
Yield: 3 to 4 servings

1 pound lean ground beef
⅓ cup toasted sesame seeds
1 egg
⅓ cup tomato sauce
⅓ package frozen chopped onions
⅓ package frozen chopped green peppers

TRIPLE RECIPE
Yield: 8 to 10 servings

3 pounds lean ground beef
1 cup toasted sesame seeds
2 eggs
One 8-ounce can tomato sauce
One 10-ounce package frozen chopped onions
One 10-ounce package frozen chopped green peppers

Sesame seeds are often less expensive at a health food store. To toast, preheat oven to 350°F. Bake sesame seeds 3 to 5 minutes, stirring occasionally.

Mix all the ingredients in a large mixing bowl with your electric mixer. (There is no need to thaw frozen onions and peppers.) Pat into a loaf shape and bake at 350°F for 40 minutes, less for smaller size loaves. Divide meat into meal- or individual-size portions, if that meets your needs. Bake that part you need immediately and freeze the remainder.

TO SERVE WHEN FROZEN. You may bake the loaves straight from the freezer. Allow 15 to 30 minutes extra baking time, depending on the thickness of your meatloaf.

THREE-IN-ONE MEATLOAF (COUNTRY PATÉ)

Paté is just a fancy word for meatloaf. When you serve this, add some class and call it Country Paté. Remember, any leftovers make great sandwiches; they're also good warmed up with mashed potatoes.

SINGLE RECIPE *Yield: 4 to 5 servings*	DOUBLE RECIPE *Yield: 8 to 10 servings*
½ pound lean ground beef	1 pound lean ground beef
½ pound ground veal	1 pound ground veal
½ pound lean ground pork	1 pound lean ground pork
1½ teaspoons salt	1 tablespoon salt
½ teaspoon freshly ground pepper	1 teaspoon freshly ground pepper
½ cup frozen chopped onions	1 cup frozen chopped onions
½ cup frozen chopped green pepper	1 cup frozen chopped green pepper
½ cup wheat germ	1 cup wheat germ
1 egg	2 eggs
1½ teaspoons Dijon mustard	1 tablespoon Dijon mustard

Preheat oven to 350°F. Combine all the ingredients in your mixing bowl. Mix well with your electric mixer, then shape into a loaf. Divide meatloaf into meal- or individual-size portions, which cook more quickly and are so convenient for those times when you need to prepare a meal for only one or two. Bake in a 350°F oven for approximately 1 hour. Pyrex custard dishes (10-ounce size) are perfect for shaping individual-size "loaves." For a more festive look, use a ring mold; unmold on a large platter and fill center with mashed potatoes or peas.

BAKED SPAGHETTI FLORENTINE

The addition of chopped spinach to this casserole dish gives it its unique flavor and appearance. It's an easy recipe to make for large groups or to put in the freezer for future meals.

Yield: 6 servings

1½ pounds lean ground beef	2 teaspoons salt
Vegetable oil, if needed	¾ teaspoon oregano
1 large Spanish onion, coarsely chopped	½ teaspoon pepper
	½ teaspoon garlic powder
2 celery ribs, chopped	¾ pound very thin spaghetti
One 2-pound 3-ounce can Italian style tomatoes, or 2½ pounds fresh tomatoes, peeled and cut into wedges	One 10-ounce package frozen chopped spinach, thawed
	½ cup Parmesan cheese

In a large skillet, brown meat in oil, if needed. When meat has lost its pink color, add onion and celery and continue cooking over moderately high heat for about 5 minutes, stirring constantly. Add tomatoes and seasonings and bring to a boil. Lower heat, cover, and simmer for 1 hour.

Meanwhile, cook spaghetti according to package directions, drain thoroughly, and set aside. When sauce is done, add cooked spaghetti and thawed package of frozen spinach. Mix thoroughly. Pour into a lightly buttered 9 × 13-inch casserole and sprinkle top with grated Parmesan cheese. Bake in a preheated 350°F oven for 30 minutes, or until hot and bubbly.

BARBECUED SHORT RIBS

These ribs can be cooked on a grill or in your oven, whichever you prefer. They are very tender and lean and have a nice spicy flavor. Because they are precooked, the actual broiling time is quite short.

Yield: 6 servings

3 pounds boneless beef short ribs	1½ teaspoons salt
½ cup dry red wine	2 tablespoons cider vinegar
One 8-ounce can tomato sauce	1 tablespoon Dijon mustard
1 tablespoon dehydrated minced onions	Dash cayenne

Remove any excess fat from ribs with a sharp knife. Put in a large pot, cover with water, bring to a boil, and simmer for about 2 hours. (To make a good stock, add one or two knuckle bones, some carrots, celery tops, onions, parsley, a bay leaf, and peppercorns.) Remove ribs from stock; strain and reserve stock for future use.

Place ribs on a broiling pan or grill. Combine wine, tomato sauce, onions, salt, vinegar, mustard, and cayenne pepper. Pour over the ribs and broil or grill, basting continuously. Watch closely, as they scorch easily! When the meat seems nicely glazed, remove from oven or grill and serve with remaining sauce.

Have your butcher bone your meat for you; it's much easier this way. The next time they are on sale, you may wish to buy a large quantity of these beef ribs. Precook them all at one time and then freeze them in meal-size portions. Have your sauce in the refrigerator, and you can whip up a tasty meal in minutes.

BARBECUED ROUND BONE POT ROAST A LA ITALIENNE

Easy and inexpensive weekend fare. This economy cut of meat will be tender, even when served rare, after being properly marinated.

Yield: 6 to 8 servings

½ cup vegetable oil
⅓ cup vinegar
1 envelope (1½ ounces) dry
 spaghetti sauce mix

1 slice beef chuck arm pot roast, 3 to 4 pounds (approximately 1–1½ inches thick)

Combine vegetable oil, vinegar, and spaghetti sauce mix in a small bowl, mixing until sauce ingredients dissolve. Spear meat from both sides with a large fork so that marinade may run into it and place meat in large, flat, shallow container or plastic bag. Pour marinade over meat. Marinate 4 to 6 hours or overnight, turning meat several times. Remove from marinade and place on grill or broiler pan about 3 to 4 inches from heat. Broil or grill about 10 minutes on each side for medium rare, basting with remaining marinade.

SHERRIED BEEF

While this dish is easy enough to prepare for the family, you can also enjoy serving it for guests.

Yield: 10 to 12 servings

3 pounds lean stewing beef, cut into
 1-inch cubes
Two 10¾-ounce cans cream of
 mushroom soup
1 pound fresh mushrooms, sliced

¾ cup dry sherry
¼ cup dry onion soup mix
Parsley
1 tablespoon flour (optional)

Combine first five ingredients (except parsley and flour) in a large casserole. Cover and bake in a preheated 325°F oven for 3 hours, or in a 300°F oven for 4 hours. In slow cooker, cook on low for 6 to 8 hours. Garnish with parsley sprigs. Good served over buttered noodles, rice, or toast.

If you like a thicker gravy, remove some of the juice in the pan, cool, and add flour, mixing well. Return this mixture to pan. Continue cooking and stirring until gravy becomes thicker.

BEEF FONDUE

Let your guests do the cooking with this easy and fun way of entertaining.

When preparing beef fondue you must have a fondue pot. Usually they are made out of metal or enamelware. You cannot use a crockery fondue pot that was designed for cheese fondue. Don't try to serve more than six, or at the most eight, people with a single fondue pot (less if you don't have an electric pot). When the pot is overcrowded, forks become entangled and food is lost in the cooking oil. All this diminishes the fun of fondue eating.

HOW MUCH TO FIGURE PER PERSON. This depends. If you are serving your fondue as a main meal, usually one-third pound of boneless meat per person is quite sufficient. When serving beef fondue as a snack or light supper, one-fourth pound per person should be ample; as an appetizer much less is needed.

My favorite cut of meat for this dish is beef loin tenderloin steak. Although it may seem rather extravagant when priced per pound, it figures somewhat less when you realize it is completely boneless and fat free, leaving absolutely no waste. Beef round tip steak or roast, rib eye, beef loin T-bone steak, and porterhouse steak are other suitable selections. Be sure to remove all fat and bones from the meat. Figure only on the weight of the lean meat when figuring the number of servings. Cut meat into approximately 1 × 1½-inch chunks.

When you serve beef fondue as a main meal, the only accompaniments that are necessary, along with the sauces, are a loaf of sliced French or Italian bread, butter, and a large tossed salad, generally with a vinegar and oil dressing.

When you serve fondue as a snack or light supper, the salad is not necessary, but you still may wish to add other accompaniments, such as sweet pickled onions, marinated mushrooms, and kumquats.

HOW IT'S DONE. Set the table, have the meat cut up, sauces prepared, and other accompaniments ready. (Have salad assembled, but do not toss until the last minute.)

Just before serving, heat 2 cups of peanut or vegetable oil, or half oil and half butter, in your electric fondue pot. If your fondue pot is heated with alcohol or sterno, heat the oil on your stove to a temperature of 375° to 400°F. Transfer heated oil to your fondue burner, toss the salad, and call your guests.

Each person takes a number of meat pieces on his or her plate, spears each with his fondue fork, and cooks it to his preference (rare, medium, or well done). Serve one or all three sauces, as you prefer.

FONDUE ETIQUETTE. The fondue forks are never put to the diner's mouth. Instead, the cooked meat is removed from the fondue fork to the diner's own plate. Guests should be careful to shake off all grease so as not to spatter the tablecloth when retrieving meat from the fondue pot. A fun thing to mention is that anyone who loses his or her meat in the pot owes the host and hostess a bottle of wine. Or as some have it, the ladies owe a kiss and the men a bottle of wine.

3-In-1 Sauce for Beef Fondue

This fondue sauce comes to us from a Swiss friend. It's easy to prepare three different sauces from a single base. Also, the addition of beaten egg whites makes the sauce light, yet creamy, and also low in calories.

SINGLE RECIPE
Yield: Approximately 6 servings

2 egg whites
1 cup mayonnaise
½ teaspoon curry (or to taste)
Dijon mustard
2 cloves garlic, minced

2 teaspoons capers, chopped
1 small dill pickle, chopped, or 1
    rounded tablespoon piccalilli sauce
1 tablespoon chopped parsley

Beat egg whites until quite stiff and gently fold in mayonnaise. Now divide this mixture into three serving bowls. (Usually the tartar sauce goes first, so I make a little bit more of this.) In the first bowl add the curry sauce, mixing well. The amount of curry may be increased or decreased according to taste. For a more spicy flavor, add a pinch or two of hot Madras curry powder.

In the second bowl add 1 rounded teaspoon of the Dijon mustard. Again, this may be increased or decreased according to your taste. However, the sauces should be a little on the strong side. An alternate sauce can be made with horseradish: add a rounded teaspoon or two of creamy horseradish to egg white and mayonnaise mixture.

For the tartar sauce in the last bowl, press 2 cloves of garlic, add the capers, chopped pickle, and parsley and mix. Refrigerate all three bowls until serving time.

Other condiments that go well with beef fondue are sweet and/or sour pickled onions, watermelon rind pickles, kumquats, sliced dills, and chutney.

VARIATIONS. Shelled and deveined shrimp may be served along with the beef. The shrimp is delicious with the sauces. However, it does require a little longer cooking time, depending on the size of the shrimp.

Chicken breasts, boned and cut into chunks, are especially good with the curry sauce.

Oriental Sauce

Yield: ¾ cup

½ cup mayonnaise
¼ cup dairy sour cream
¼ cup chopped green onion

1 tablespoon soy sauce
1 teaspoon ground ginger

Mix all ingredients together in a bowl, store in covered container, and refrigerate until serving time.

IRISH BRISKET STEW IN CLEAR BROTH

This simple one-pot meal is easy on the cook, as well as the pocketbook. A tasty treat the whole family will enjoy when served with crusty hot bread and butter.

Yield: 10 to 12 servings

1½-2 pounds lean beef brisket
Water
Celery greens
1 large onion, sliced
2 sprigs parsley
Large clove garlic
1 bay leaf
10 peppercorns
3 medium carrots

One 9-ounce package frozen french green beans
12 small new potatoes, peeled
3 ribs celery, sliced horizontally
One 1-pound can stewed tomatoes (optional)
½ cup frozen chopped green peppers
2 tablespoons instant beef bouillon granules
Pepper to taste

Put beef brisket in a large kettle or slow cooker and cover with sufficient water to make about 3 quarts. (Usually about 2 quarts of water are needed.) Add celery greens, sliced onion, parsley tops, and seasonings and simmer for 3 hours or until tender. Do not boil. When meat is tender, remove from heat and cool slightly. Remove any scum or fat from top of broth. Unless meat is very fatty, it will not be necessary to cool broth to remove fat. Strain broth. Return only meat and broth to kettle. Add remaining vegetables and instant bouillon granules and simmer for an additional hour until vegetables are done. Taste liquid and if more salt or pepper is needed, add additional bouillon granules or pepper. Serve with horseradish or mustard sauce (see page 91).

This stew freezes well. However, remove potatoes before freezing.

RANCHO GRANDE STEAK

An economical, as well as delicious, way of serving steak to a large number of people. Leftover meat and au jus gravy makes marvelous French Dip Sandwiches.

Yield: 8 to 10 servings

4 pounds boned top round steak, cut 2 inches thick
One 1$^{1}/_{16}$-ounce package seasoned beef marinade
$^{3}/_{4}$ cup dry red wine

3 tablespoons lemon juice
2 tablespoons salad oil
$^{1}/_{2}$ teaspoon freshly ground pepper
$^{1}/_{2}$ teaspoon dried rosemary

Wipe meat with a damp cloth. Combine all the remaining ingredients in a flat container large enough to hold the meat. (I use a plastic pie-taker.) Pierce all surfaces of the meat thoroughly with a sharp pick or fork. Baste marinade over the meat and let stand for 15 minutes, turning and basting the meat several times. Brown meat in an electric skillet at 400°F for 5 minutes on each side (using a minimum amount of shortening). After the meat is well browned, reduce heat to 325°F and continue cooking for 10 minutes on each side for rare. Add an additional 5 minutes for medium rare. Remove meat from skillet and slice into thin slices across the grain diagonally.

To grill on the barbecue, sear meat for 5 minutes on each side. Then raise grill about 2 inches and continue cooking as per above directions.

French Dip Sandwiches

Heat and cut leftover Rancho Grande Steak on wooden carving board that has a well in it to collect all the natural juices.

Heat french rolls slightly in microwave oven or wrapped in foil on grill or in regular oven. Cut in half with a bread knife and dip cut sides of rolls into au jus. Slice meat very thin and stack on bottom half of rolls; cover with top half that has also been dipped into juice and serve immediately. They are especially good served with coleslaw (see page 134).

HAM

Every busy person should become acquainted with the many "admirable" characteristics of ham. Because it can be served warm or cold, it is the perfect entrée for casual summer or winter serving and entertaining. Most hams are precooked and need only a short time in the oven when heated. You may wish to serve a canned ham, a rolled boneless ham, or a regular ham, either cut in half or whole, depending on the number of people you are serving and the size of your family. Do buy enough ham so that you can have some planned leftover meals. Some of my favorite dishes are made with leftover ham. The following recipes can be made from leftover ham. They are often more delicious than the original sliced hot or cold ham.

Other recipes for leftover ham are: Polynesian Ham Salad (see page 138); Lentil Soup (see page 77); Bean Soup (see page 76); Ham Casserole (see page 68); Hungarian Potato Casserole (see page 94); Egg-stuffed Tomatoes (see page 119); Pineapple-Ham Sandwich Filling (see page 56); Fettucine Alla Papalina (see page 68).

HUNGARIAN STYLE HAM AND POTATO CASSEROLE

An old world recipe with old world flavor, made simply with modern ingredients for the cook of today. This delectable casserole can be made with baked or broiled ham leftovers or boiled ham.

At your delicatessen counter ask for boiled ham ends. These are the end pieces from a canned ham that did not make full slices. They are sold at quite a savings and are a marvelous buy for this type of dish.

Yield: 1½-quart casserole; 6 to
8 servings

1 cup commercial sour cream or sour half-and-half	4 cups frozen hashed brown potatoes
3 tablespoons onion soup mix (approximately ½ package)	3 hard-cooked eggs, sliced
1 cup milk	1½ to 2 cups cooked ham, diced, sliced, or ground
½ teaspoon salt	Bread crumbs
Pepper to taste	Butter

Blend sour cream with onion soup mix (just as it comes from the package). Then add milk and seasonings. Grease a 1½-quart casserole and arrange in layers one-third of the potatoes, one sliced egg, one-third of the sour cream mixture, and one-third of the ham. Repeat layering. Top with bread crumbs and dot with butter. Bake in a 350°F oven for 30 minutes, or until bubbly.

HAM AND SPANISH RICE–STUFFED GREEN PEPPERS

Green peppers are a marvelous source of vitamin C. Stuffing or filling green peppers seems to be a favorite way of serving them. I think you'll enjoy this quick and easy recipe using Spanish Rice mix. Make them in quantity and freeze for future meals. Small households can halve or quarter recipe.

Yield: 8 large or 12 medium size
stuffed peppers

8 large or 12 medium size green peppers
1 cup boiling water
One 6-ounce package Spanish rice mix
2 tablespoons butter

2 cups ground cooked ham
1 can (1 pound) stewed tomatoes
One 8-ounce can tomato sauce with onions
Bread crumbs
Butter

Cut the tops off the green peppers and save. Remove the seeds and blanch peppers in boiling water for 5 minutes. (When doing a large batch, have a large kettle half filled with boiling water. Put in only enough green peppers at a time so that they are at least half filled with boiling water.) Meanwhile, pour 1 cup boiling water over rice and let stand for 12 minutes. Add butter. Then combine remaining ingredients except bread crumbs and butter in a large mixing bowl. Add rice. After the peppers have been blanched and drained, cool sufficiently to handle. Stuff green peppers with ham-rice mixture. Sprinkle lightly with dry bread crumbs and top with butter. Then add green pepper tops.

VARIATION. If you desire a gravy or sauce with your stuffed peppers, use 1 can of tomato soup, diluted with only ½ can of milk or half-and-half. Mix thoroughly and pour into bottom of baking dish.

TO FREEZE. Set tray of green peppers in freezer. When they are completely frozen, wrap either individually or in family-size portions in plastic or heat-and-seal bags or heavy duty foil. Seal, label, date, and return to freezer.

TO BAKE UNFROZEN (WHEN YOU HAVE JUST PREPARED THEM). Place peppers upright in a covered casserole dish and bake in a moderately hot oven (375°F) for 30 minutes. Uncover casserole for last 10 minutes to brown.

TO BAKE FROZEN. Follow the above instructions and add 25 minutes to the baking time.

HAM LOAF WITH PINEAPPLE GLAZE

A marvelous way to use any leftover ham. Ham Loaf can be made up into one large loaf or several small or individual ones, making it a handy dish for the small household, as well as the large.

SINGLE RECIPE
   Yield: One 2-quart loaf

1 pound ground cooked ham (about 4 cups)
½ pound ground beef
1 cup bread crumbs
¾ cup milk
1 egg

¼ cup chopped onions (frozen or fresh)
¼ cup snipped parsley
1 teaspoon dry mustard
Freshly ground pepper

Combine all the ingredients, mixing thoroughly. Pack lightly into a 2-quart loaf pan or baking dish. Bake uncovered in a moderate 325°F oven for 45 minutes. Remove drippings with a baster and invert onto an ovenproof platter. Brush with Pineapple Glaze and arrange pineapple slices attractively on top. Return to oven for 15 minutes.

Pineapple Glaze

One #2 can (1-pound 4-ounce) sliced pineapple
¼ cup brown sugar
1 teaspoon dry mustard

Drain juice from pineapple and reserve liquid. Combine ½ cup of pineapple liquid with brown sugar and mustard. Bring to a boil until sugar is dissolved and continue boiling for about 5 minutes. Brush this mixture onto the ham loaf after it has been inverted, and arrange pineapple slices attractively on top of loaf. May also be garnished with cloves and/or place a few maraschino cherries, cut in half, in center of pineapple slices for added color.

HUNGARIAN PORK CHOPS

An all-in-one type of dish that's easy to prepare.

SINGLE RECIPE
   Yield: 3 servings

3 thick butterfly pork chops from which most of the fat has been removed
1½ teaspoons vegetable oil
½ cup frozen chopped onions
¼ cup dry white wine
½ teaspoon dill seed
1 teaspoon caraway seeds

DOUBLE RECIPE
   Yield: 6 servings

6 thick butterfly pork chops from which most of the fat has been removed
1 tablespoon vegetable oil
1 cup frozen chopped onions
½ cup dry white wine
1 teaspoon dill seed
2 teaspoons caraway seeds

¼ teaspoon salt
⅛ teaspoon garlic powder
One 8-ounce can sauerkraut
½ cup dairy sour cream or sour
    half-and-half
1 teaspoon paprika

½ teaspoon salt
¼ teaspoon garlic powder
One 16-ounce can sauerkraut
1 cup dairy sour cream or sour
    half-and-half
2 teaspoons paprika

In a large frying pan or electric skillet, slowly brown chops on both sides in oil. Pour off drippings. Add onions and seasonings, along with sauerkraut. Lower heat and cover. Simmer for about 35 minutes or until pork chops are done. Add sour cream, mixing well. Simmer for an additional 5 minutes.

OKTOBERFEST SKILLET DINNER

Serve in large portions because the tantalizing aroma of this dish will really increase those already hearty fall appetites. It is easy to prepare, as neither potatoes nor apples need peeling.

Yield: About 5 servings

1¼ pounds German smoked sausage
2 tablespoons butter
10 small new potatoes
¼ cup dry white wine or water

6 large or 10 medium size tart
    cooking apples
⅓ cup brown sugar
One 1-pound can sauerkraut

Cut the sausage in angle-shaped pieces. Sauté briefly over moderate heat in butter. Meanwhile, scrub new potatoes well, leaving skins on, and add them to the sausage. Add water or wine, lower heat, cover with lid, and simmer until potatoes are almost tender. Meanwhile, core and quarter apples. If the apples are very large, cut into eighths. When the potatoes are almost done, add apples, brown sugar, and sauerkraut. Stir and cover, cooking until apples are tender. Stir often so the sugar will caramelize and leave a thin coating over the rest of the ingredients. When apples are done, serve immediately.

DILLED PORK ROAST

This is a marvelous and easy way to prepare pork roast. It makes great leftovers; you can also use thin slices on sandwiches, hot or cold.

SINGLE RECIPE
    Yield: 5 servings (about ⅓
    * pound per person)*

One 2- or 3-pound boned and
    trimmed loin pork roast
1 can (10¾ ounces) chicken broth,
    undiluted

1 teaspoon dried dill
1 tablespoon paprika
1 medium size onion, sliced finely

Place pork roast in slow cooker. Cover with chicken broth. Sprinkle with dill, paprika, and onion. Cover and cook on low for 6 hours. Cool. Remove any fat from juices. Slice meat finely. Return to juices and warm for serving. It may be served without chilling. However, it does slice better when chilled.

LAMB AND VEAL

LAMB SHISH KEBABS

Excellent served with wild rice or Wild Rice Casserole (see page 102).

Yield: 5 to 6 servings

1¾ pounds leg of lamb, cut into 1½-inch cubes (remove all membrane)
1 medium size yellow onion, grated
¼ cup oregano (fresh, crumbled leaves, not powdered), or 1 teaspoon dried oregano
1 teaspoon salt
1 teaspoon thyme

2 cloves garlic, minced
¼ cup snipped parsley
One 8-ounce can tomato sauce
¼ cup vegetable oil
Small 1-inch white onions
Whole mushrooms
Green pepper squares
Cherry tomatoes

Combine all the ingredients except vegetables and marinate meat overnight in refrigerator, or for 6 to 7 hours at room temperature. Place meat on skewers and barbecue or broil with direct heat (about 3 inches from heat) for 12 to 15 minutes. Lamb should be slightly pink in center.

Also fill a few skewers with small 1-inch white onions (parboil so they will be done at the same time as the other vegetables), whole mushrooms, green pepper squares, and cherry tomatoes.

VEAL FLORENTINE

A favorite for the homemaker who serves dinner at different times during the evening. Just slip prepared dish under the broiler and *voila,* dinner is served! Elegant enough for company.

Yield: 6 servings

6 veal cutlets (about 1¼ pounds)
1 egg
¼ cup milk
Bread crumbs
4 tablespoons butter
One 10-ounce package frozen creamed spinach, cooked

Pinch nutmeg
2 slices Swiss cheese for each cutlet
2 teaspoons Parmesan cheese
One 8-ounce can tomato sauce, optional

Pound veal cutlets until very thin. Dip in egg and milk mixture and then into fine bread crumbs. Let rest for 15 to 20 minutes. (If you are doing this earlier in the day, refrigerate until ready to cook.) Sauté in 3 tablespoons of butter about 5 minutes on each side, or until brown. Transfer cutlets in a single layer onto a large baking sheet or platter. Thaw and heat spinach according to package instructions. Place hot creamed spinach on top of veal cutlets. Cover each cutlet with two slices of Swiss cheese and sprinkle Parmesan cheese over each cutlet. Place under broiler until bubbly; serve immediately. When serving on individual plates, put a few tablespoons of warmed tomato sauce on the bottom of each plate before adding the cutlets. This is best prepared on oven-proof plates, so that each individual plate can be put under the broiler for the few minutes necessary to heat it.

LAMB PILAF

A marvelous all-in-one-dish with a distinctive Mediterranean flavor.

SINGLE RECIPE	DOUBLE RECIPE
Yield: 3 to 4 servings	*Yield: 6 to 8 servings*
2 tablespoons butter or margarine	4 tablespoons butter or margarine
1½ pounds boned lean lamb, cut into 1-inch cubes	3 pounds boned lean lamb, cut into 1-inch cubes
1 small Spanish onion, sliced thinly and separated into rings	1 large Spanish onion, sliced thinly and separated into rings
¼ teaspoon cinnamon	½ teaspoon cinnamon
¼ teaspoon pepper	½ teaspoon pepper
½ cup raw rice	1 cup raw rice
½ cup white raisins	1 cup white raisins
½ teaspoon salt	1 teaspoon salt
1 cup consommé (omit water)	1 can (10¾ ounces) consommé
2 tablespoons lemon juice	1 cup water
½ cup (one 3-ounce package) sliced almonds, toasted	¼ cup lemon juice
¼ cup chopped or snipped parsley	1 cup (two 3-ounce packages) sliced almonds, toasted
	½ cup chopped or snipped parsley

Preheat oven to 400°F. Melt half the butter or margarine in a large heavy skillet. For a single recipe sauté half the lamb over very high heat until browned. Remove lamb from skillet and drain on paper toweling. Remove excess fat from the skillet. Add remaining butter or margarine and repeat with remaining lamb. Lower heat. Sauté onions. Add cinnamon and pepper and continue cooking over medium low heat for 3 to 5 minutes, until the onions become soft. For a double recipe butter a 2½-quart casserole lightly. Sprinkle the bottom with ¼ cup of raw rice and ¼ the raisins, meat, and onions. Repeat layers. Sprinkle top with salt. Add combined consommé (and water for double recipe). Pour over the mixture along with lemon juice. Cover. Bake at 400°F for 50 minutes. Remove cover. Sprinkle top with almonds and parsley. Bake 10 minutes longer. Serve immediately.

TO FREEZE. Arrange Pilaf in casserole dish, omitting almonds and parsley. Do not bake. Freezer-wrap, label, date, and freeze.

TO SERVE WHEN FROZEN. Bake frozen casserole in a preheated 400°F oven for 1 hour and 35 minutes. Or thaw and follow above instructions. Remove cover, add almonds and parsley, and continue baking for another 10 minutes. Smaller casserole dishes require less baking time.

POULTRY

Poultry has long been the budget-stretching friend of the cook. It's nutritious—an excellent source of protein, yet low in calories and cholesterol for those on diets. Serve it often, but in different ways.

If your family likes only certain parts of the chicken, it may be more economical to buy only these pieces. However, you usually pay premium prices for selected parts. I buy whole fryers, cut up, reserve the choice pieces which the family enjoys most, and put the rest of the bird into a large kettle. Cover it with water and add celery greens, parsley, a bay leaf, peppercorns, cut-up carrots, and some onion slices (no salt). I usually add an extra breast or thigh to the pot to ensure an adequate quantity of boned chicken. Simmer gently for 2 hours or until meat falls off the bones. Strain broth. Cool and remove meat from the bones; put into freezer cartons. If you intend to store the meat for long periods, pour a small quantity of broth over the meat, date, label, seal, and freeze. Now you'll have a quantity of boned, cooked chicken in your freezer to use in the many recipes that call for it. Remember that chicken and turkey may be interchanged in almost any recipe. All this can be done at your convenience. Just put less favorite chicken parts in plastic bags and freeze until you have time.

Freeze broth in cartons or ice cube trays. When freezing in cartons, make sure you leave ample head room. Again date and label, then freeze. Put filled ice cube trays in freezer until frozen. Remove frozen broth-cubes and put into plastic freezer bags that have been dated and labeled. These little cubes are marvelous to have on hand when making sauces and gravies and cooking vegetables.

TANGY BARBECUED CHICKEN

This barbecued chicken has a citrus-like tang.

Yield: 4 servings

One 3½-pound frying chicken, cut up

One 6-ounce can (⅔ cup) lemonade concentrate

2 teaspoons Worcestershire sauce

2 tablespoons soy sauce

1 teaspoon garlic powder

¼ teaspoon white pepper

Wash chicken and drain on absorbent paper. Combine all the remaining ingredients and marinate chicken for at least ½ hour before barbecuing, turning several times. Chicken can marinate in refrigerator all day if you wish. Barbecue over moderate heat for 30 minutes, turning frequently and watching closely. It may also be broiled in your oven broiler.

SCALLOPED CHICKEN

This elegant yet budget-priced meal may be served to company and family alike. It's also a good way to use any leftover turkey you might have stashed away in your freezer.

Yield: 6 to 8 servings

3 cups boned chicken

8 ounces fresh mushrooms, sliced

4 ounces butter

4 cups bread stuffing cubes

2 tablespoons milk

1 tablespoon minced dry onions

¾ teaspoon poultry seasoning

½ teaspoon salt

Freshly ground pepper to taste

4 ounces shredded Swiss cheese

2 tablespoons butter or chicken fat

2 tablespoons flour

3 cups chicken broth

Preheat oven to 325°F. Arrange chicken in the bottom of a 2½-quart casserole (or several small ones, if desired). Wash and slice mushrooms (use the slicing blade on your food processor if you have one). Sauté mushrooms in butter and add to bread cubes, along with drippings in pan. Add milk, onions, seasonings, and cheese and mix lightly with a fork. (This mixture will not be moist.) Spread over chicken layer in casserole. Now make a gravy by melting butter or chicken fat and adding flour. When thoroughly incorporated, add chicken broth and cook until thick and bubbly, stirring constantly. Pour the chicken gravy over the chicken and dressing mixture. Bake uncovered in a 325°F oven for 45 to 50 minutes or until dressing is brown and crusty.

SESAME BAKED CHICKEN

I can't imagine cooking fried chicken any way other than in the oven. There's no watching, no spattering, no muss or fuss, and fewer calories. Prepare enough for one meal and have a few pieces left over for lunch-box treats or snacks of cold chicken. The sesame seeds give it a crispy, nutty flavor. If you don't have biscuit mix, flour will do nicely; however, you'll get a lighter and crispier crust with the mix.

Yield: 6 servings

Two 3-pound fryers, cut up
1 cup flour or biscuit mix
½ cup sesame seeds
2 teaspoons salt
Freshly ground pepper

½ teaspoon ginger
2 eggs
¾ cup milk
2 tablespoons vegetable oil, if
  necessary

Wash chicken parts and pat dry with a paper towel. Set aside necks, backs, and gizzards to be cooked for chicken broth (see page 100). Combine biscuit mix or flour, sesame seeds, and seasonings in a plastic bag. Shake well to mix. In a blender or mixing bowl combine eggs and milk and pour into a shallow bowl. Dip chicken pieces in egg and milk mixture and then shake well in plastic bag to cover with flour and sesame seed mixture. Lay in a large, generously greased baking dish or pan and let set for about 15 minutes before baking. Bake with skin side down at 425°F for 35 minutes until chicken is nicely browned on underside. Turn chicken pieces and return to oven for another 25 minutes or until chicken is done and crispy brown all over. Serve immediately while hot.

A very good milk gravy can be made from pan drippings. Add a tablespoon or two of leftover flour mixture and stir until dissolved. Set baking pan over moderate heat, add milk, and continue stirring and cooking until all the drippings are dissolved and the gravy is thick and smooth. Salt with beef bouillon granules (see page 74).

WILD RICE CASSEROLE

This marvelous dish, which can be made with chicken breasts or turkey leftovers, is good for guests and family alike.

Yield: 8 servings

One 6-ounce package Uncle Ben's
  Wild Rice (or Drumstick Rice)
1 cup instant rice
1 pound bulk pork sausage
One 4-ounce can sliced mushroom

caps, or ½ pound fresh
  mushrooms
2 cans (10¾ ounces) cream of
  mushroom soup, undiluted

1 teaspoon Worcestershire sauce	1½ cups dry bread cubes or broken
2 large chicken breasts, sliced, or 12	sliced bread
slices turkey breast	¼ cup butter, melted

Cook wild rice as directed on package. Also, separately cook 1 cup instant rice. Combine. Sauté sausage in a skillet for 5 minutes over medium heat until brown. Pour off fat, continue stirring, and break into small pieces, again pouring off any excess fat. Add mushrooms, soup, and Worcestershire sauce. Toss mixture lightly with cooked rice. Spoon half the rice mixture into a generously greased 2-quart casserole (or two 1-quart or four 1-pint casseroles). Add chicken breasts or sliced turkey. Top with remaining rice mixture and cover with bread cubes. Drizzle melted butter over bread and bake uncovered at 375°F for 30 minutes. This casserole can be prepared in advance. If stored in the refrigerator, bake for 1 hour.

TO FREEZE. Prepare as above but do not bake; freezer-wrap, date, label, and freeze.

TO SERVE WHEN FROZEN. It is best to thaw in refrigerator overnight or at room temperature for several hours. Then follow the above baking instructions.

CHICKEN CASSEROLE

Because it is so simple and *must* be prepared ahead of time, this dish is great for casual entertaining, as well as for serving to your family on busy days. Served with rolls, cranberry relish or sauce, and a vegetable, this will make a marvelous supper menu.

SINGLE RECIPE
Yield: 4 to 5 servings

1 cup cooked chicken, cut up
Half a 7-ounce package Creamettes or elbow macaroni
One 10¾-ounce can cream of chicken soup, undiluted
1 cup milk
¼ pound shredded sharp Cheddar cheese
2 tablespoons chopped frozen onions
2 tablespoons chopped green pepper
One 2-ounce jar pimiento, chopped
Half a 6-ounce can (or a whole can if you wish) water chestnuts, sliced
Salt and pepper to taste

DOUBLE RECIPE
Yield: 8 to 10 servings

One 7-ounce package creamettes or elbow macaroni
2 cups cooked chicken, cut up
Two 10¾-ounce cans cream of chicken soup, undiluted
2 cups milk
½ pound shredded sharp Cheddar cheese
¼ cup chopped frozen onions
¼ cup chopped green pepper
One 4-ounce jar pimiento, chopped
One 6-ounce can water chestnuts, sliced
Salt and pepper to taste

Place elbow macaroni in the bottom of a large mixing bowl or a lightly greased baking dish (approximately 9 × 13 inches). Mix chicken with remaining ingredients. Stir gently until well blended. Cover and let casserole sit overnight in the refrigerator. Bring casserole to room temperature before baking. Bake uncovered at 350°F for approximately 1 hour.

TO FREEZE. Because this recipe makes such a large quantity, you might care to divide it up into smaller portions and freeze them. Let ingredients set in refrigerator overnight and then freeze. Thaw completely before baking.

POACHED CHICKEN BREASTS

An economical entrée with great taste appeal. Terrific for waist-watchers, too.

SINGLE RECIPE	TRIPLE RECIPE
Yield: 2 servings	*Yield: 6 servings*
1 large chicken breast, boned and halved	3 large chicken breasts, boned and halved
¾ cup fresh mushrooms, sliced	½ pound fresh mushrooms, sliced
⅓ cup plain yogurt	One 8-ounce container plain yogurt
1 tablespoon dehydrated beef mushroom soup mix	3 tablespoons dehydrated beef mushroom soup mix

Preheat oven to 350°F. Arrange chicken breasts in a glass 9 × 13-inch baking dish. Sprinkle with mushrooms. Combine yogurt with dehydrated soup mix and spread over top of chicken breasts. Cover dish with foil and bake in a 350°F oven for 25 minutes.

The sauce in which these chicken breasts are cooked is especially delicious and would be a very low-calorie topping for baked or boiled potatoes. Remember, half a medium size baked potato has only about 65 calories. It's not the potato, but what you put on it and how it's prepared that adds the additional calories. However, be cautious and don't overdo the carbohydrate bit.

SEAFOOD

Nutritionists are constantly telling us how good fish and seafood are for us, and that we are not getting sufficient amounts of it in our diets. Dietitians remind us what a marvelous type of food this is for those of us who are calorie- and cholesterol-watchers. Economists keep telling us what a marvelous buy it can be for the budget-watchers, especially frozen fish. So all in all, this food comes highly recommended by many sources. With improved shipping techniques, seafood and fish consumption is steadily growing. We as a nation are developing a taste for fish and seafood. Because fish is always cooked quickly, it's perfect for the busy person.

On the following pages are some unusual and delicious, yet very simple to prepare, recipes that you'll want to serve year round.

CRISP OVEN-FRIED FISH

This is much easier, quicker, and less fattening than the old top-of-the-stove method. If you're cooking for a large group, such as for a fish fry, you may prepare several pans at once in your oven.

SINGLE RECIPE
Yield: 3 servings

2 tablespoons milk
1 beaten egg
1 pound thawed fish fillets, steaks or
  small whole fish
½ cup corn meal, crushed corn
  flakes, or crushed potato chips
⅛ teaspoon thyme
2 tablespoons Parmesan cheese
  (optional)
3 tablespoons melted butter
Parsley and lemon

DOUBLE RECIPE
Yield: 6 servings

¼ cup milk
1 beaten egg
2 pounds thawed fish fillets, steaks,
  or small whole fish
1 cup cornmeal, crushed corn flakes,
  or crushed potato chips
¼ teaspoon thyme
¼ cup Parmesan cheese (optional)
⅓ cup melted butter
Parsley and lemon

QUADRUPLE RECIPE
Yield: 12 servings

½ cup milk
2 beaten eggs
4 pounds thawed fish fillets, steaks,
  or small whole fish
2 cups cornmeal, crushed
 corn flakes, or crushed potato chips

½ teaspoon thyme
½ cup Parmesan cheese (optional)
⅔ cup melted butter
Parsley and lemon

Preheat oven to 500°F. Combine milk and egg. Dip fish in mixture and then into seasoned crumbs. Let stand for about 15 minutes. Place a single layer of fish in a buttered baking dish. Sprinkle with any remaining crumbs and drizzle with melted butter. (Parmesan cheese may be mixed with crumbs or sprinkled on top.) Bake for 12 to 15 minutes or until tender and flaky. No need to turn fish. Don't overbake, or fish will become dry. Garnish with parsley and lemon wedges. Serve with tartar sauce or Quick Almond Butter Sauce, p. 107.

SPAGHETTI WITH CLAM AND SHRIMP SAUCE

A very simple meal to prepare. This clam sauce with shrimp added is one of the best I've ever tasted.

Yield: 5 to 6 servings

8 ounces spaghetti	2 teaspoons cornstarch
1 tablespoon olive oil	One 10-ounce package thawed
One 8-ounce can minced clams	frozen shrimp, peeled and
½ cup (1 stick) butter	deveined
2 cloves garlic, pressed	White pepper
3 scallions, chopped	Salt
2 tablespoons parsley, snipped	2 tablespoons Parmesan cheese

Cook spaghetti in hot boiling water, to which 1 tablespoon of olive oil has been added. (Water should continue boiling rapidly throughout cooking time.) Cook until spaghetti is just tender.

Meanwhile, drain clams, reserving liquid. Add enough water to the liquid to measure 1 cup. In a large skillet melt 6 tablespoons of the butter. Add pressed garlic, scallions, and parsley and sauté until onions are clear. Combine cornstarch with reserved clam juice and add to the onion mixture. Cook over medium heat, stirring constantly until thickened and smooth. Simmer for an additional 2 minutes. Add clams and shrimp. (If shrimp are very large, cut into smaller pieces.) Heat through and continue cooking until shrimp are pink and firm. (Do not overcook or shrimp will toughen.) Adjust seasoning, adding white pepper to taste.

Drain spaghetti, toss with remaining butter, Parmesan cheese, and a light touch of salt. Arrange on a warm serving platter and pour the sauce over the top. Garnish with additional parsley sprigs, if you wish.

FILLET OF SOLE IN WINE SAUCE

Although this recipe calls for fillet of sole, any filleted fish (whatever the sportsman in your family has in your freezer) may be substituted. The sophisticated homemaker who is looking for quick gourmet meals that are easy on the pocketbook, as well as light on the calories, will get raves from this one.

Yield: 4 to 6 servings

1 cup clam or Clamato juice	1 large clove garlic, split
½ cup dry white wine	2 pounds fillet of sole
1 bay leaf	Lemon juice
6 whole black peppercorns	2 tablespoons butter
½ teaspoon salt	2 tablespoons flour
Generous sprig of fresh dill or	White wine
parsley	Chopped parsley

Preheat oven to 350°F. Combine clam juice, wine, bay leaf, pep-percorns, salt, dill, and garlic in a saucepan and bring to a boil. Reduce heat and simmer, uncovered, for 15 minutes. If you are using frozen fillet of sole, thaw completely. Dry with paper towels. Then in a large 9 × 13-inch baking dish form fillets into rolls, putting the dark side down. Arrange in a single layer. Sprinkle generously with lemon juice. Strain clam broth over fillets. Cover dish tightly with foil or lid and bake in 350°F oven for 30 minutes. With a slotted spoon remove fillets into a bake-proof serving dish. Melt butter in a saucepan or microwave oven and add flour, mixing until thoroughly blended. Pour broth into this and cook until thickened. If mixture becomes too thick, thin with additional white wine. Pour sauce over fish and keep warm in oven at low temperature until serving time. Sprinkle with chopped parsley just before serving.

VARIATION. Toasted sliced almonds may also be sprinkled over the fish.

SALMON PATTIES

These salmon patties can be mixed the night before.

Yield: 6 to 8 small patties

8-ounce can red Sockeye salmon	½ cup corn flake crumbs
1½ tablespoons dry minced onions	2 tablespoons vegetable oil
2 eggs, beaten	Lemon wedges
Pinch baking soda	Parsley
1 heaping tablespoon sour cream	

Remove skin and bones from salmon; do not drain liquid. Flake salmon in mixing bowl; add onions and eggs, beating well into mixture. Add baking soda, sour cream, and corn flake crumbs, again mixing well. Refrigerate for about 30 minutes.

In a large heavy skillet, heat oil until quite hot. Form salmon mix-ture into patties and brown in hot oil, turning once. When done, re-move patties onto absorbent paper. Place on serving platter, garnish with lemon wedges and parsley, and serve immediately. These patties, when served cold, make a very good sandwich.

QUICK ALMOND BUTTER SAUCE FOR FISH

This easy and delectable sauce is quickly prepared in your blender.

Yield: Approximately 1 cup

¼ pound butter

2 egg yolks

½ teaspoon dry mustard

Dash cayenne

2 tablespoons lemon juice

1 tablespoon hot water

1 tablespoon dry sherry

½ cup toasted sliced almonds

Melt butter and continue cooking over moderate heat until butter turns golden brown. In your blender or food processor combine egg yolks, mustard, cayenne, and lemon juice. When blended, slowly pour the warm amber-colored butter into the blender in a thin stream, blending at low speed. When completely incorporated, add hot water and sherry. If mixture is too thick, add another tablespoon of hot water. Remove from blender and combine with toasted almonds. Serve separately or pour over broiled or baked fish. Although it is best served with salmon, halibut, or trout, it is also good with walleye and turbot.

Vegetables, Pastas, and Rice

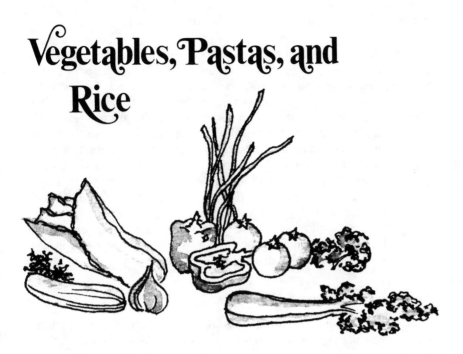

Handling and Storing Vegetables

Be generous with the amount of vegetables you include in your menu planning. Whether they are fresh or frozen makes little difference. A recent research project at Stanford Research Institute stated that frozen vegetables outranked fresh vegetables in the nutrient department. The reason for this is that vegetables harvested for freezing are fully vine-ripened, then flash-frozen within hours of picking. Produce picked in volume in distant fields is hydrocooled in the field, then rushed to a temperature- and humidity-controlled site for washing, sizing, packing, and freezing. Locally packed produce doesn't undergo this field-to-market cooling which is so important in preserving the vitamin content of our fresh produce. This study showed, for instance, that frozen brussels sprouts contained 27 percent more vitamin C than fresh brussels sprouts. Frozen lima beans were 36 percent higher in vitamin A than the fresh product found in your local produce market. Frozen spinach had 212 percent more vitamin C than fresh!

This study shows how important it is that we handle our fresh produce properly, whether it is purchased at market or picked from your garden. Letting fresh produce sit in a hot car for even just an hour is going to affect the quality enormously. Take a cooler along in your car and store your fresh produce and frozen foods after shopping when the weather is terribly hot or you have a long drive home. When you take your vegetable purchases home, whether fresh or frozen, be sure to store them properly and promptly.

Fresh produce should be washed and well dried, then placed in a plastic bag or tight-fitting container and stored in the crisper of your refrigerator. Some vitamins, such as vitamin C, can easily be destroyed by exposure to air, so proper wrapping before refrigeration is vital. Don't cook more vegetables than you expect to use at one meal. Left-over vegetables that are kept in the refrigerator for several days can lose as much as one-half to two-thirds of their vitamin content. Reheating will result in additional loss. Some vitamins are water-soluble, so cook vegetables in a minimum amount of water or steam them. Don't soak fresh vegetables in water to crisp them; instead, sprinkle with water and wrap well in damp towel, plastic bag, or foil.

When you wish to substitute fresh vegetables for frozen vegetables called for in a recipe, or vice versa, remember that you will lose several ounces in cleaning and trimming fresh vegetables.

Shortcuts in Preparing Vegetables

One of the most common mistakes the American cook makes when preparing vegetables is overcooking them. When you cook fresh vegetables, such as broccoli, cauliflower, string beans, and spinach, a good method to use is to pour about a half cup of hot water over the vegetables; use more water only when cooking a very large quantity. Cover and bring to a quick boil over high heat. If you are using an electric stove, turn off the heat when the vegetables come to a full boil and set your timer for 10 minutes; keep covered and do not remove lid until timer rings. The heat in the electric coils will continue cooking the vegetable for a few minutes longer and the steam will continue cooking them until the time is up. Drain vegetables; pour sauce, seasonings, or butter over vegetables. Your vegetables should be just crispy tender and very tasty.

If you have a gas stove, bring the vegetables to a full boil and cook for 3 minutes; turn the heat off and let the vegetables set on the stove for another 7 minutes. Don't remove the lid during this time, as that allows steam to escape. Drain and serve.

CARROTS. Carrots are much easier to slice, dice, or cut into julienne pieces after they are cooked rather than before. Slice them diagonally with a crinkle cutter into attractive shapes. It takes about a fraction of the time to do this after they are cooked than it would if done beforehand.

LEFTOVER VEGETABLES. Leftover vegetables can easily be marinated (see page 142). Put warm leftovers in marinade and let set on kitchen counter for an hour. Then refrigerate and serve several days later. This is especially helpful for the small family that normally has vegetables left over. If you have a large family, cook twice as many vegetables, serve half of them in the normal manner that your family enjoys, and marinate the remainder for another meal.

RAW VEGETABLES. Raw vegetables are good served with a dip (see pages 145 and 146). Not only is this a very healthful way of eating vegetables, but also it is easy on the cook. An assortment of vegetables can be cleaned, cut, and refrigerated in plastic bags. At serving time, simply arrange them on a platter with the dip in the center of the platter. Raw vegetables are usually a welcome change. This is also a good way of getting rid of dibs and dabs of raw vegetables in your refrigerator. Recommended vegetables for eating raw are carrot and celery sticks, julienne slices of green pepper, cauliflower, radishes, green onions, cucumber sticks, and cherry tomatoes.

ASPARAGUS TO ZUCCHINI

ASPARAGUS ALMONDINE

Just great for fresh, tender asparagus stalks.

Yield: 4 to 6 servings

One 1-pound bunch fresh asparagus
3 tablespoons butter
¼ cup toasted sliced blanched
  almonds

¼ teaspoon salt
2 teaspoons lemon juice

Wash fresh asparagus and snap off tough stem ends. Line asparagus in a row on your chopping board and slice diagonally into 1-inch lengths. Drop into 2 quarts of rapidly boiling water and cook for 3 to 5 minutes until just crispy tender. (The taste test is the only way to be sure. Cooking time also depends on how thick the asparagus stalks are. Thin ones cook much quicker.) Drain and arrange on serving platter. Melt butter and add toasted almonds, salt, and lemon juice. Stir for 1 minute and pour over hot asparagus, toss, and serve immediately.

ASPARAGUS CASSEROLE

Great for entertaining, as it can be made ahead.

SINGLE RECIPE
Yield: 2 to 3 servings

One 10-ounce package frozen
  asparagus pieces or 10–12 ounces
  fresh asparagus, cut up
1½ tablespoons margarine
1½ tablespoons flour
½ cup milk
¼ teaspoon salt
¼ cup grated American cheese
1 cup fresh pulled bread crumbs in
  fairly large chunks

DOUBLE RECIPE
Yield: 4 to 6 servings

Two 10-ounce packages frozen
  asparagus pieces, or about 1½
  pounds fresh asparagus, cut up
3 tablespoons margarine
3 tablespoons flour
1 cup milk
½ teaspoon salt
½ cup grated American cheese
2 cups fresh pulled bread crumbs in
  fairly large chunks

Cook fresh asparagus until barely tender or thaw frozen asparagus. Meanwhile, make sauce by melting margarine and adding flour, stirring until smooth. Add milk; continue cooking over moderate heat, stirring all the while, until mixture is thick and smooth. Add grated cheese and seasonings. Fold in asparagus and bread crumbs and pour into a 1½-quart flat casserole. Bake in a preheated 350°F oven for 30 minutes.

ASPARAGUS GRANDÉ

The wheat germ adds a nice nutty flavor to the asparagus.

SINGLE RECIPE	DOUBLE RECIPE
Yield: 2 servings	*Yield: 4 servings*
½ pound asparagus	1 pound asparagus
1½ tablespoons butter or margarine	3 tablespoons butter or margarine
2 teaspoons wheat germ	1 tablespoon wheat germ

Wash asparagus gently and thoroughly, break off ends, and either lay flat in a large skillet or cooking utensil, or tie, stand upright, and steam in a tall blanching or steaming kettle. Cook asparagus rapidly for 5 to 7 minutes (if stalks are quite thick, 10 minutes may be necessary), until ends of stalks are crispy tender. Don't overcook; asparagus should not be soft. Drain. Melt butter in skillet or microwave oven, add wheat germ, and continue cooking until wheat germ is lightly browned. Sprinkle over cooked asparagus and toss until lightly covered with buttered wheat germ.

GREEN BEANS WITH FRENCH FRIED ONIONS

If you're tired of serving your vegetables the same old way, here's a quickie that's sure to make a hit.

SINGLE RECIPE
Yield: 6 to 8 servings

One 9-ounce package frozen French style green beans	One 3½-ounce can French fried onions
1 tablespoon butter	Salt to taste

Prepare green beans according to package directions. Drain and toss with butter until it is melted. Combine beans with French fried onions in a 1-quart serving dish, toss gently, and salt to taste. Serve.

"BAKED" BEANS

An excellent recipe for doctoring up the regular canned pork and beans. A real time-saver and great to take along on picnics and pot-luck dinners.

Yield: 6 to 8 servings

Two 1-pound cans pork and beans	5 drops Worcestershire sauce
¼ cup brown sugar	½ cup catsup
1 teaspoon prepared mustard	3 or 4 slices bacon

Mix all ingredients except bacon in an oven-proof bowl or casserole dish. Lay bacon slices over top. Bake uncovered 2½ to 3 hours at 325°F.

BRUSSELS SPROUTS WITH PECANS

A tasty, yet easy way of serving this vegetable.

Yield: Approximately 8 servings

Two 10-ounce packages frozen brussels sprouts, or 2 pints fresh brussels sprouts	½ cup chopped pecans
	¼ cup butter
	1 tablespoon dehydrated onions
1 cup chicken bouillon or chicken stock	¼ cup snipped parsley
	Pimiento strips
½ teaspoon salt	

Cook frozen brussels sprouts according to package directions. If using fresh vegetables, wash and trim sprouts. Place in pan, add stock and salt, and bring to a boil. Cover and simmer for 10 to 15 minutes until tender, but still crisp. Drain, reserving liquid, and keep hot. Meanwhile, in a shallow skillet sauté pecans in butter, adding onions and about ¼ cup of the reserved bouillon. Pour over the brussels sprouts and toss lightly. Sprinkle with parsley and garnish with a few pimiento strips.

GLAZED CARROTS

Add variety to your meals by serving these quick and easy Glazed Carrots.

SINGLE RECIPE	DOUBLE RECIPE
Yield: 2 servings	*Yield: 4 servings*
About ⅓ pound small tender carrots	About ⅔ pound small tender carrots
1 tablespoon orange marmalade	2 tablespoons orange marmalade
1½ teaspoons butter	1 tablespoon butter
1½ teaspoons parsley, snipped	1 generous sprig parsley, snipped

Scrape or peel carrots. If they are small and tender, leave whole. If larger, slice them diagonally in ¾-inch slices. In appropriate size sauce pan, put ½ cup water, cover and cook until tender (about 10 to 15 minutes after water boils). Drain well. Add marmalade and butter, mixing until well blended. Lower heat and simmer for about 10 minutes, turning carrots occasionally, so they will be well glazed. Sprinkle with snipped parsley. Serve immediately.

CAULIFLOWER WITH CHEESE AND SESAME SEEDS

This quickie has a wonderful blend of flavors: the nutty taste of toasted sesame seeds mixed with cheese and sour half-and-half.

SINGLE RECIPE	DOUBLE RECIPE
Yield: Approximately 3 servings	*Yield: Approximately 6 servings*
½ medium head cauliflower	1 medium head cauliflower
Salt and pepper to taste	Salt and pepper to taste
½ cup sour half-and-half	1 cup sour half-and-half
1½ cups shredded sharp Cheddar cheese	2 or 3 cups shredded sharp Cheddar cheese
2 teaspoons toasted sesame seeds	1 tablespoon toasted sesame seeds

Wash and separate the cauliflower into flowerettes. Place in the saucepan. Add ⅓ cup of water. Bring to a boil. Put lid on and steam until just tender. Remove from pan and drain. Place in 1- or 1½-quart casserole dish or baking dish. Sprinkle with salt and pepper. Spread with sour half-and-half (to cut calories, use half yogurt). Sprinkle with cheese and top with sesame seeds. If your dish is small, make two layers, using half the sour half-and-half and half the Cheddar cheese. Bake in a preheated 350°F oven for 30 minutes.

CELERY CHINOISE

For variety, here's a recipe that is quick to prepare, yet quite different.

Yield: 3 to 4 servings

3 cups celery (approximately 7 stalks)	2 cups fresh mushrooms, sliced
	⅓ cup slivered almonds, toasted
3 tablespoons butter	Salt and pepper to taste

Remove and wash the large, coarse, outer stalks from your celery. Slice diagonally into thin strips, sufficient to make 3 cups of celery. Simmer in ½ cup water until just tender (approximately 3 minutes after the water has begun to boil). Meanwhile, melt butter and sauté mushrooms in skillet. When celery is crispy tender, drain thoroughly and add to mushrooms, tossing well. Now add toasted almonds, salt and pepper to taste, and serve immediately.

BARBECUED CORN ON THE COB

A great way to serve corn on the cob to a large group. Everything can be prepared in advance, and there is no messy buttering of the corn after it is served.

Yield: 1½ dozen ears

1½ dozen ears of corn
1 stick butter, melted
½ package dehydrated onion soup
  mix

½ teaspoon garlic salt

Clean corn. Twirl melted butter, onion soup mix, and garlic salt in blender or food processor. Generously brush butter-onion mixture onto corn with a pastry brush. Wrap each ear individually with foil. Refrigerate until ready to cook. Bake in 375°F oven or roast on the grill for approximately 30 minutes. Serve immediately.

When serving smaller or individual quantities, butter as many ears as you wish and refrigerate remaining onion-garlic butter for future use. Corn ears can also be wrapped in clear plastic and cooked in microwave oven.

SAUTÉED CUCUMBERS

You'll be amazed at how good sautéed cucumbers taste. In our country, cucumbers are traditionally served raw or marinated; this recipe is a delightful change.

SINGLE RECIPE	DOUBLE RECIPE
Yield: 2 to 3 servings	*Yield: 4 to 6 servings*
1 medium size cucumber, pared and sliced	2 medium size cucumbers, pared and sliced
½ teaspoon salt	1 teaspoon salt
1 tablespoon butter or margarine	2 tablespoons butter or margarine
¼ teaspoon dried tarragon	½ teaspoon dried tarragon

Sprinkle salt over sliced cucumbers and let stand for 30 minutes. Squeeze excess moisture from cucumbers. In a medium size saucepan melt butter and add squeezed cucumbers and tarragon. Sauté over moderate heat uncovered for about 10 minutes. Serve.

DEVILED EGGPLANT

This is one of the most delicious vegetable dishes I've tasted in a long time. It makes a marvelous entrée for meatless meals.

Yield: 8 servings as a vegetable,
   less for a meatless entrée

1 large eggplant, peeled
1 teaspoon salt
½ teaspoon pepper
3 tablespoons salad oil or olive oil
1 cup frozen chopped onions
2 cloves garlic, pressed or minced
2 cups fresh peeled tomatoes, chopped, or one 16-ounce can seasoned stewed tomatoes

Pinch thyme
¼ cup snipped parsley
½ cup bread crumbs
Salt
Pepper
1 cup grated cheese: Swiss, Gruyère, mozzarella, or jack cheese

Peel and slice the eggplant in eight 1-inch-thick slices. With a sharp knife cut down until they are all of uniform circumference; reserve any trimmings and leftover eggplant. Place on a large, round, oven-to-table, oiled baking dish. Sprinkle with salt and pepper. Broil for 5 minutes on each side. While the eggplant slices are broiling, sauté onions in oil until yellowed. Add the minced garlic and continue sautéing for another few minutes; add tomatoes. Coarsely chop reserved eggplant trimmings and add to tomato mixture. Continue cooking over low heat until mixture has thickened slightly. Stir in thyme, parsley, and bread crumbs. Add salt and pepper to taste. Spoon vegetable mixture on top of broiled eggplant circles. Top with cheese and bake in 350°F oven until cheese has melted.

POACHED ONIONS

Instead of serving fried or French fried onions with your steak or liver, try these. They're really good and have fewer calories.

SINGLE RECIPE
   Yield: 2 or 3 servings

1 large Spanish onion
1 teaspoon bouillon granules
¼ cup water
Salt and pepper to taste

DOUBLE RECIPE
   Yield: 6 servings

2 large Spanish onions
2 teaspoons bouillon granules
½ cup water
Salt and pepper to taste

Peel onions and slice into ¼-inch slices. In a large skillet, dissolve bouillon granules in water. Add onions, bring to a rapid boil, lower heat, cover, and simmer about 10 to 15 minutes or until onions are yellow and limp. Drain and season to taste. Serve.

FRENCH BAKED POTATOES

Instead of French frying these delicate potato chips, they are baked at a high temperature with a small amount of butter. They become deliciously crispy and may be topped with cheese if you wish. (These are so good, there never seems to be enough.)

Yield: About 4 servings

3 large or 4 medium-size Idaho baking potatoes	Salt and pepper
	Basil
2 tablespoons butter or margarine, melted	½ cup grated Swiss cheese (optional)

Preheat oven to 450°F. Peel potatoes and slice them with the slicer in your food processor. Place the potato slices in the bottom of a 9 × 13-inch baking dish, overlapping them in rows. Pour melted butter over the potato slices; sprinkle generously with salt and pepper and several pinches of basil. Bake at 450°F for approximately 20 minutes. The degree of crispness desired will vary from family to family; also, some potatoes will have more moisture content than others, so check potatoes for crispness. You may wish to leave them in for another few minutes for extra crispy potatoes.

CHEESE TOPPING. If cheese topping is desired, remove potatoes from oven after 20 minutes or after desired crispness is achieved. Sprinkle with Swiss cheese that has been grated in your food processor, and return them to oven for an additional 5 minutes, or until cheese is melted and bubbly.

MEXICAN POTATOES

Try these Mexican Potatoes for added zip. They're great with steak or other broiled meats.

SINGLE RECIPE	DOUBLE RECIPE
Yield: 2 to 3 servings	*Yield: 4 to 6 servings*
4 medium size potatoes	8 medium size potatoes
1 medium size tomato	2 medium size tomatoes
1 tablespoon vegetable oil	2 tablespoons vegetable oil
½ teaspoon cumin seed	1 teaspoon cumin seed
½ teaspoon salt	1 teaspoon salt
¼ teaspoon turmeric	½ teaspoon turmeric
Pinch red pepper flakes	¼ teaspoon red pepper flakes
4½ teaspoons butter	3 tablespoons butter

Peel potatoes and place in cold salted water. Cover and bring to a boil. You can cook potatoes and then peel, if you wish. Simmer until tender, but not soft. (Be careful not to overcook.) Drain and let cool long enough so that they can be handled. Cut potatoes into 1-inch cubes. While the potatoes are cooking, prepare the tomatoes by dipping them for a half-minute in boiling water, then peeling. Set aside. In a large skillet heat vegetable oil and add seasonings, stirring until well blended. Toss in potatoes and add butter, one teaspoon or tablespoon at a time. When the mixture is well blended and all the potatoes are coated, lower heat. Dice peeled tomatoes and add to potatoes along with seasonings. Toss gently. Remove from heat, cover, and let stand until ready to serve. This dish should be served hot.

SPINACH SQUARES WITH HOLLANDAISE SAUCE

Although it doesn't take long to put this dish together, it can be made in advance and refrigerated until just before serving time

Yield: 9 generous servings

Two 10-ounce packages frozen chopped spinach
1 cup frozen chopped onions
2 tablespoons butter, margarine, or olive oil
3 eggs

1⅔ cups milk
½ teaspoon seasoned salt
2 cups soft bread crumbs (3 slices of bread)
Double recipe Quick Hollandaise Sauce

Heat packages of frozen spinach in microwave oven or follow directions for cooking on package. Drain well. Meanwhile, in skillet sauté onions in butter, margarine, or olive oil until clear and tender. In blender combine eggs, milk, and seasoned salt. Pour into a generously greased 9 × 9-inch baking dish. Add onions, spinach, and bread crumbs, mixing well. Bake in a preheated 350°F oven for 40 to 45 minutes, or until set. Remove from oven and serve immediately, spooning a generous portion of Hollandaise Sauce over each square.

Quick Hollandaise Sauce

This tastes every bit as good as authentic Hollandaise sauce, but it has fewer calories, is less expensive, and is much simpler to make.

*Yield: Enough sauce for 1 or 2
packages of frozen vegetables*

4 tablespoons mayonnaise
1 tablespoon lemon juice
2 tablespoons butter or margarine

1 egg yolk
Dash cayenne pepper
Dash salt

Cook your vegetables in the bottom of a double boiler. Five minutes before they're done, put top on double boiler. Combine mayonnaise and lemon juice in top and stir until well blended. Let cook about 3 minutes, until fairly warm; then add butter or margarine and egg yolk, stirring constantly. When mixture is thick, add seasonings; stir and remove from heat. Drain vegetables, arrange on serving plate, and cover with sauce. Sauce may also be cooked over low direct heat.

Serve over green vegetables. This yellow sauce helps make an attractive vegetable platter. It is especially delicious served over broccoli, artichoke hearts, asparagus, or cauliflower, or as a dip for whole artichokes.

EGG-STUFFED TOMATOES

Particularly nice when field-grown tomatoes are available. Makes a very good meatless entrée.

SINGLE RECIPE	DOUBLE RECIPE
Yield: 3 servings	*Yield: 6 servings*
2 hard-cooked eggs	4 hard-cooked eggs
2 tablespoons finely chopped celery	¼ cup finely chopped celery
1 tablespoon sour cream or sour half-and-half	2 tablespoons sour cream or sour half-and-half
1 round teaspoon mayonnaise	1 tablespoon mayonnaise
½ rounded teaspoon dehydrated minced onion	1 rounded teaspoon dehydrated minced onion
1 teaspoon prepared mustard	2 teaspoons prepared mustard
1 teaspoon Worcestershire sauce	2 teaspoons Worcestershire sauce
¼ teaspoon salt	½ teaspoon salt
Pepper to taste	Pepper to taste
3 medium size tomatoes	6 medium size tomatoes

Chop eggs finely or put through mouli grater or food processor using metal blade. Add remaining ingredients except tomatoes and mix well. Chill until serving time.

Cut tomatoes petal fashion into sixths toward the stem end, leaving all portions attached at the base. Open the petals and fill with egg mixture. Set on a bed of lettuce and garnish with watercress or parsley and radish roses, if desired. Olives would also make a nice garnishment for this dish.

VARIATION. One cup of cooked ham, shrimp, or other seafood can be added to the egg mixture for a more substantial meal.

QUICK YAMS L'ORANGE

If your family likes yams or sweet potatoes, this is a real quickie recipe for dressing them up.

Yield: About 4 servings

2 tablespoons butter
⅓ cup orange juice
⅓ cup Cointreau or orange liqueur
Dash nutmeg and cloves

One 1-pound can yams, drained and
sliced, or 3 medium size yams,
cooked, peeled, and sliced (or
sweet potatoes)

In a medium size skillet melt butter, add orange juice, orange liqueur, and spices, mixing well. Add the drained and sliced yams and cook over moderate heat for about 10 to 15 minutes, or until yams are well coated and candied. Serve immediately.

ITALIAN ZUCCHINI (A LA PROVENCALE)

An interesting vegetable casserole which will add variety to your meals. A single recipe makes a rather generous amount. Divide into smaller quantities if you wish; serve one now and freeze remainder.

SINGLE RECIPE
Yield: 3 to 4 servings

¼ cup rice
½ cup boiling water
½ teaspoon beef bouillon granules
2 small size zucchini
½ medium size Spanish onion
½ clove garlic, pressed
Olive oil
One 1-pound can stewed tomatoes
2 tablespoons snipped parsley
Parmesan cheese

DOUBLE RECIPE
Yield: 6 to 8 servings

½ cup rice
1 cup boiling water
1 teaspoon beef bouillon granules
3 medium size zucchini
1 medium size Spanish onion
1 clove garlic, pressed
Olive oil
Two 1-pound cans stewed tomatoes
¼ cup snipped parsley
Parmesan cheese

Cook rice until light and fluffy in boiling water, to which bouillon has been added. Meanwhile, slice zucchini and onions into ¼-inch slices. Sauté zucchini in olive oil with onion slices and garlic. In a 9 × 13-inch oven-proof casserole dish (or 9-inch pie plate for single recipe), arrange a layer of zucchini and onion mixture, alternating with cooked rice and then tomatoes, until all the ingredients have been used. Sprinkle top of casserole with parsley and Parmesan cheese and bake uncovered in a preheated 375°F oven for about 20 to 25 minutes, or until mixture is bubbly.

TO FREEZE. After casserole has been assembled, cover tightly and freeze.

TO SERVE WHEN FROZEN. Thaw at room temperature and bake according to above instructions.

ZUCCHINI CON TOMATO

This very tasty vegetable dish is a modern adaptation of an old Italian recipe.

SINGLE RECIPE
Yield: 4 servings

2 cups zucchini
¼ cup water
One 8-ounce can stewed tomatoes
½ cup canned pizza sauce
1 tablespoon plus 1 rounded
  teaspoon minced onions, or 1½
  teaspoons dried minced onions
¼ pound Cheddar cheese, coarsely
  grated

DOUBLE RECIPE
Yield: 8 servings

4 cups zucchini
½ cup water
One 1-pound can stewed tomatoes
One 8-ounce can pizza sauce
3 tablespoons minced onions, or 1
  tablespoon dried minced onions
½ pound Cheddar cheese, coarsely
  grated

Wash and slice zucchini into ¼-inch slices. Boil gently in small amount of salted water until crispy tender, about 5 minutes. Drain and place in buttered 2-quart casserole dish for a single recipe. Add tomatoes, pizza sauce and onions; then top with grated cheese. Bake in a preheated 350°F oven for 30 minutes.

VARIATION. Add 1½ pounds lean ground beef, which has been browned with onion. This makes it a complete meal.

PASTAS AND RICE

We have the Italians to thank for their many pastas and the endless variety of sauces to serve with them. Add variety to your meals by serving some of these tasty and authentic Italian provincial sauces. Usually they require a minimum of preparation time.

Rice, although a staple of the far and near east for centuries, has been adopted by most western cultures. For variety, try some of the recipes included in this section.

CREAMY SPAGHETTI

For a creamy and delicious pasta, serve this dish which is easily made ahead of time. It freezes well.

SINGLE RECIPE
Yield: 3 servings

¼ pound linguine
2 ounces cream cheese, softened
½ cup cottage cheese
2 tablespoons sour cream or sour
  half-and-half
2 tablespoons chopped fresh chives,
  or 1 round teaspoon dried chives
2 tablespoons bread crumbs
1½ teaspoons melted butter

DOUBLE RECIPE
Yield: 6 servings

½ pound linguine
4 ounces cream cheese, softened
1 cup cottage cheese
¼ cup sour cream or sour
  half-and-half
¼ cup chopped fresh chives, or 1
  tablespoon dried chives
¼ cup bread crumbs
1 tablespoon melted butter

QUADRUPLE RECIPE
Yield: 12 servings

1 pound linguine
1 8-ounce package cream cheese,
  softened
2 cups cottage cheese
½ cup sour cream or sour
  half-and-half

½ cup chopped fresh chives or 2
  tablespoons dried chives
½ cup bread crumbs
2 tablespoons melted butter

Cook linguine in a large kettle (5 to 6 quarts for large recipe) of boiling salted water until *al dente;* drain. Meanwhile, cream the cream cheese until soft and fluffy. Add cottage cheese and continue mixing. Now add sour cream and chopped chives. Pour over well drained and hot linguine and toss. Pour into a buttered 2-quart casserole dish. Combine bread crumbs with melted butter. Sprinkle over the top of linguine and bake in a preheated 350°F oven for about 25 to 30 minutes. Serve immediately.

MACARONI AND CHEESE CASSEROLE

This creamy and nutritious dish is bound to be a hit. It has a delicious crusty, cheesy top. If you have been serving your family prepared (either frozen or boxed) packages of macaroni and cheese, be prepared for an avalanche of requests for seconds.

Yield: About 1½ quarts

One 7-ounce package elbow
  macaroni
2 cups cottage cheese, large or small
  curd
1 cup dairy sour cream or sour
  half-and-half

1 egg, slightly beaten
¾ teaspoon salt
1 tablespoon prepared mustard
10 ounces sharp Cheddar cheese,
  shredded

Preheat oven to 350°F. Cook macaroni according to package directions. In a large mixing bowl combine cottage cheese, sour cream, egg, salt, and mustard and mix well. Coarsely shred Cheddar cheese, using your food processor if you have one, reserving about 2 ounces for the topping. Combine the rest of the Cheddar cheese with the cottage cheese mixture. Add hot drained macaroni to the cheese mixture and mix well. Pour into a greased 1½-quart casserole dish, top with reserved Cheddar cheese, and bake uncovered at 350°F for 45 minutes.

SPANISH RICE

Make this simple recipe in large quantities, so you will have enough for more than one meal. It is particularly good served with pork chops or pork roast.

Yield: 5 to 6 cups

½ pound bacon, diced (optional)
One 10-ounce package chopped frozen onions
One 10-ounce package chopped frozen green peppers
1 cup uncooked rice (or ½ cup long grain white rice and ½ cup brown rice)

One 1-pound can seasoned stewed tomatoes
One 6-ounce can tomato paste
One 10-ounce can chicken broth, undiluted
Pinch sage
½ teaspoon salt
Pepper to taste

Cook diced bacon in a large skillet or microwave oven until crisp. Remove bacon and reserve. Drain some of the bacon fat, leaving just enough to sauté onions and green pepper. (Substitute 2 to 3 tablespoons of vegetable oil if you do not wish to use bacon.) Sauté for about 3 minutes. Add rice and continue cooking until white rice turns slightly brown. Add remaining ingredients and bring to a boil. Cover, reduce heat, and simmer for 45 minutes (when using brown rice), or just 20 minutes when using white rice alone. Add bacon bits and serve immediately.

TO FREEZE. Pack in freezer containers or heat-and-seal bags and freeze immediately.

TO SERVE WHEN FROZEN. When it is packed in freezer containers, thaw at room temperature or in refrigerator. Preheat oven to 350°F. Place rice mixture on a large cookie sheet, sprinkle with 1 to 2 tablespoons of water, and bake at 350°F until heated through. When it is packed in heat-and-seal bags, simply place in boiling water and continue cooking until rice mixture is heated through, or heat in covered dish in microwave oven.

RISOTTO (ITALIAN RICE)

Add variety to your meals with this unusual rice dish.

Yield: 6 to 8 servings

2 tablespoons butter or margarine
2 tablespoons olive oil
¾ cup chopped frozen onions
⅓ cup chopped frozen green peppers
1 clove garlic, minced
½ cup long grain rice
½ cup brown rice
3½ cups chicken or beef broth (or
  use two 10¾-ounce cans
  condensed beef broth and add
  sufficient water to make 3½ cups)

2 teaspoons beef bouillon granules
Salt to taste
½ cup Parmesan cheese
1 tablespoon butter

In a large, heavy skillet or Dutch oven that has a tight-fitting lid, combine butter and olive oil, heating until butter is melted. Sauté onions and green pepper until onions are golden brown. Now add garlic and rice and continue cooking, stirring constantly, until white rice takes on a brown color (about 3 to 5 minutes). Add broth and bouillon granules, bring to a boil, stir, and cover with lid. Lower heat and continue cooking for about 30 minutes or until liquid is completely absorbed. (Do not stir.) When rice is done and liquid has been absorbed, add salt, cheese, and additional butter. Toss and serve immediately.

MADRID STYLE RICE

This is a marvelous recipe to keep in mind for those occasions when you have a lot of rice left over and you don't know what to do with it. This happened to us recently when we had an impromptu supper with friends and ordered chop suey from the local take-out. It seems they always supply about three times the quantity of rice needed. It is against my better principles to throw anything out.

Yield: 6 to 8 servings

3 cups cooked rice
½ cup boiling water
2 teaspoons bouillon granules
3 green onions, finely chopped
1 clove garlic, minced or pressed
4 medium size tomatoes, peeled and
  coarsely chopped, or 1 cup tomato
  purée

One 4-ounce can roasted and peeled
  green chilies, chopped
¼ cup snipped parsley or fresh
  coriander
One 2-ounce jar pimientos, chopped
2 tablespoons butter
Salt and pepper to taste

In a large skillet combine rice with boiling water in which bouillon granules have been dissolved. Continue cooking over moderate heat and add onions, garlic, tomatoes, chilies, parsley, and pimiento. Cover and simmer for about 20 minutes. Add butter and more water if needed. There should be no liquid remaining when the rice is served. Season with salt and pepper according to taste.

LAYERED HAMBURGER-NOODLE BAKE

This easy meal-in-one-dish is so versatile. Make it ahead of time and divide it into several smaller containers, freezing some for future meals. (Larger households may wish to double the recipe.) It tastes good reheated in your microwave oven.

Yield: 2 quarts, or 6 servings

4 ounces medium wide egg noodles
1 pound lean ground beef
One 15-ounce can tomato sauce
1 teaspoon sugar
½ teaspoon salt
¼ teaspoon garlic salt
¼ teaspoon pepper
One 8-ounce package cream cheese,
   softened
½ cup sour cream or sour
   half-and-half or substitute yogurt
   or cream cheese lite (Neufchatel)
   for less calories

3 tablespoons milk
2 tablespoons finely chopped onion
One 10-ounce package frozen
   chopped spinach, cooked and
   drained
½ cup shredded natural Cheddar
   cheese, mozzarella, or Swiss
   cheese

Cook noodles in a large amount of boiling salted water until tender (about 10 minutes) and drain. Brown meat in skillet, and drain off fat. Add tomato sauce, sugar, salt, garlic salt, pepper, and cooked noodles; mix and set aside. Stir together cream cheese, sour cream, milk, and onion (this can be done in your food processor or blender very quickly).

If you have a microwave oven, cook your chopped spinach in the package in your microwave oven. Lightly grease a 2-quart casserole (or several smaller casseroles equaling 2 quarts), and layer half of the ground beef mixture in the bottom of each casserole. Add half the cream cheese mixture, all of the spinach, all the remaining noodle mixture, then the other half of the cream cheese mixture. Cover and bake in a preheated 350°F oven for 40 minutes, or until bubbly. Uncover and sprinkle with Cheddar cheese. Continue baking an additional 10 minutes or until cheese is melted.

TO FREEZE. Any casserole that you wish to freeze, prepare as above, omitting Cheddar or other cheese topping. Seal and freeze.

TO SERVE WHEN FROZEN. It is best to thaw your casserole entirely in your refrigerator or microwave oven and cook according to the above instructions, adding grated Cheddar or other cheese topping during the last 10 minutes of baking.

MOTHER'S DUMPLINGS

For variety make these dumplings; they take less time to make than potatoes!

SINGLE RECIPE
Yield: 5 servings

1 cup flour (not sifted)
1 tablespoon baking powder
½ teaspoon salt

6 or more tablespoons cold milk or water

With a fork mix flour, baking powder, and salt thoroughly. Add sufficient liquid to make a soft dough. Drop by tablespoonfuls in hot stew, gravy, or broth. Steam *covered* for just 10 minutes. (Do not lift lid or peek during the 10-minute cooking interval.) There must be plenty of gravy, and it should be bubbling to cook the dumplings properly.

VARIATION. Snipped parsley, freeze-dried or fresh chives, grated cheeses, or other spices may be added to vary the flavor. Parsley and a pinch of sage added to dumpling batter is very good with stewing chicken or chicken soup.

SPAGHETTI, OIL, AND GARLIC (OLIO E AGLIO)

Simple and oh so good!

Yield: 6 servings

1 pound spaghetti
4 cloves of garlic
¼ cup olive oil

¼ cup butter (half a stick)
Salt and pepper to taste
Grated Parmesan cheese

Cook spaghetti in a large container of boiling salted water until it is tender, making sure not to overcook. While the spaghetti is cooking, crush garlic cloves and sauté in olive oil for 3 or 4 minutes over moderate heat. Discard garlic, add butter, and continue cooking until all the butter is melted. When spaghetti is *al dente,* remove from heat and drain promptly. Pour hot garlic mixture over spaghetti and season to taste with salt and pepper; toss. Serve with freshly grated Parmesan cheese or toss ½ cup of the cheese over the spaghetti mixture and serve with additional cheese.

NOODLES ALFREDO

Impress your family and friends with this quickie. For real pizazz, prepare at the table.

SINGLE RECIPE
*Yield: 4 to 6 servings (2 to 3
servings if used as entrée)*

6 cups water
6 teaspoons instant bouillon granules
One 8-ounce package medium width
  egg noodles
¼ cup butter (half stick)
1 clove garlic, pressed

⅔ cup half-and-half
¾ cup freshly grated Parmesan
  cheese
Salt and pepper to taste
Snipped parsley

Combine water and bouillon granules and bring to a boil. Cook noodles until *al dente* (usually about 10 minutes) and drain. Melt butter in a large pan and add pressed garlic; then add hot, drained noodles, toss gently to coat the noodles. Add cream and continue cooking over moderate heat or in flambé pan, tossing until the cream is completely absorbed. Remove from heat, sprinkle with Parmesan cheese, and continue tossing until all the noodles are coated. Season with salt and pepper to taste, tossing until well blended. Place in serving dish (if cooking in flambé pan, serve directly from flambé pan), garnish with snipped parsley, and serve immediately.

RICE AND BROCCOLI

This rice and vegetable combination can easily be prepared ahead of time and just popped into the oven before serving time. It is particularly good with baked or broiled meats. Make in large or small casseroles, whichever serves your family best.

*Yield: Approximately 2 quarts,
  or 6 servings*

¼ cup frozen chopped onions
½ cup chopped celery
3 tablespoons butter or margarine
One 6-ounce can water chestnuts
2 cups cooked rice
One 10-ounce package frozen
  chopped broccoli, cooked

One 10¾-ounce can cream of
  chicken soup
One 5⅓-ounce can evaporated milk
8-ounce package Cheddar cheese,
  shredded

Sauté onions and celery in butter or margarine. Slice water chestnuts in food processor or by hand. When onions are clear but not browned, add cooked rice, broccoli, cream of chicken soup, evaporated milk, and sliced water chestnuts; mix in a large bowl. Toss with one-third of the cheese. Pour into a greased 2-quart casserole or an 11¾ × 7½-inch oblong pan (or several smaller casseroles, whichever you prefer), and cover with remaining cheese. Bake in a preheated 350°F oven for 40 minutes.

Salads

For quick salads wash salad greens, dry thoroughly, and store in a plastic bag in the refrigerator. This way they will be crisp, clean, and ready for use.

The single-person or two-person household can still have a variety of salad greens. Boston and Bibb lettuce come in very small heads. Leaf lettuce and spinach can be purchased in small bunches; just ask your produce man to divide a bunch if there are no small ones. Even iceberg lettuce comes in small heads, frequently wrapped two to a package; just ask the produce person to break open the package and give you one head for half price.

Salads can be as varied as the imagination will allow. There are vegetable, fruit, poultry, seafood, marinated, tossed, molded, and combination salads, to name a few. Don't get in a rut and serve the same salad with the same dressing day in and day out. Be imaginative and serve a variety of salads.

Marinated vegetable salads are great for working people. They usually don't take long to make, and they store well in the refrigerator. There is no last minute fussing; just take it out of the refrigerator and serve.

Salads as a Main Course

Not only are salads great for calorie-counters and marvelous on the budget, but also they are chock-full of vitamins. Salads are usually simple to prepare and are often a wonderful way of using up leftover meat, cheeses, and vegetables. You are only limited by your imagination as to the type and kinds of salads you can serve.

GREEN SALADS

SALAD WITH VINEGAR AND OIL DRESSING

This is better than any bottled dressing and only takes a second longer. Have all your greens washed and crisping in the refrigerator, so that you can assemble your salad just before serving.

Lettuce (several kinds)
Green onion, snipped
Parsley, snipped
Radishes, sliced
Olive oil
Clove of garlic
Tarragon vinegar
Salt
Freshly ground pepper

USE ALL OR SEVERAL OF THE
   FOLLOWING:
Cherry tomatoes, quartered, or
   regular tomatoes cut into wedges
Artichoke hearts, cut into quarters
Anchovy fillets, chopped
Garlic or plain croutons
Marinated mushrooms (see
   page 142)

Keep a small cruet of olive oil with one clove of garlic, cut in half, soaking in it. The olive oil will have a nice hint of garlic and yet not be overpowering. You'll find many uses for this, but it is especially nice when making vinegar and oil salad dressing.

Just before serving, toss all the crisped greens, tomatoes, onions, parsley, radishes, and artichoke hearts in a large salad bowl.

Drizzle olive oil over the greens and toss gently. The greens should be just lightly covered with oil, no more. Now add anchovy fillets and pepper. Toss again, but gently, so as not to bruise salad greens. Add a few drops of tarragon vinegar; toss and taste. Add more until the right vinegar and oil combination has been achieved; it should be light on the vinegar. Add croutons and sprinkle heavily with salt. Toss, taste, and add more salt until just the perfect blending has been achieved.

Salt must always be the very last thing added to a tossed salad, as the greens will start to wilt soon thereafter. The other ingredients may be added as much as 15 minutes before serving. A common failure is not to add enough salt to cut the oil taste of the dressing, so keep a heavy hand with the saltcellar. Once you have the technique down pat, it takes no time at all to toss this salad. Practice the first time when you aren't entertaining.

ROQUEFORT DRESSING

This delicious dressing is the creamy kind you have to pay extra for in all the restaurants! Now enjoy it at home to your heart's content.

Yield: About 2 cups

6 ounces Roquefort cheese (or Blue Cheese)	Pinch cayenne
	½ teaspoon salt
4 ounces cream cheese	½ teaspoon garlic salt
5 tablespoons cream	
1 cup sour cream or sour half-and-half	

If you like a textured salad dressing, reserve approximately 2 ounces of the cheese. Put all the remaining ingredients into your blender or food processor and twirl until mixture is smooth and creamy. For added texture, add the 2 ounces of reserved cheese, crumbled.

Store in a covered container in the refrigerator. Its refrigerator life is about one week.

Generously serve this dressing over a tossed salad made with iceberg and leaf lettuce, torn. Add radish slices, tomato wedges, and cucumber slices, along with snipped green onions and parsley. No other vegetable is needed, just your meat and potatoes.

PECAN SALAD DRESSING

This simple salad dressing really gives a wonderful nutty flavor to any tossed salad.

Yield: About 2½ cups

½ cup vinegar	2 teaspoons sugar
1½ cups salad oil	½ teaspoon dry mustard
1½ teaspoons salt	½ cup chopped pecans

Whirl all the ingredients in an electric blender or food processor until mixture is emulsified, about a half-minute or so. This dressing keeps well in the refrigerator for several weeks if kept in a covered container.

WILTED SALAD

Take advantage of fresh, tender leaf lettuce when it is in abundant supply, fresh spinach, or Swiss chard. Serve good old-fashioned wilted lettuce.

*Yield: About 5 servings (for
smaller servings see notation
at end of recipe)*

1 to 1½ pounds of fresh leaf lettuce,
  spinach, or Swiss chard
¼ cup thinly sliced scallions, or 2
  tablespoons minced onions
1 tablespoon snipped fresh herbs
  (dill, garlic greens, thyme)
5 bacon slices, diced
¼ cup bacon fat

¼ cup tarragon vinegar
1 teaspoon dry mustard
1½ teaspoons sugar
¼ teaspoon salt
¼ teaspoon freshly ground black
  pepper
⅛ teaspoon garlic salt

The most important part of this recipe is to make sure that your greens are absolutely clean. Rinse them several times, swishing in the water. If you have a basket designed for this purpose, you will find the job much easier. After the greens have been thoroughly cleaned, spin dry or blot with a clean towel and refrigerate until ready to use in damp towel or plastic bag. Tear leaves into large bowl, removing coarse stems; add scallions and herbs. Fry bacon in skillet over low heat until crisp, pouring off fat as it cooks, or use your microwave oven. Drain bacon and crumble into salad bowl. Return ¼ cup bacon fat to the skillet, add vinegar, mustard, sugar, salt, pepper, and garlic salt. Bring to a boil, stirring constantly. Immediately, just before serving, pour hot dressing over salad, tossing well.

VARIATION. Several sliced radishes, cut-up tomatoes, or hard-cooked eggs may also be added.

For small or individual servings, follow recipe as given. Use only a portion of dressing on a portion of greens. Refrigerate leftover greens and dressing separately. To serve leftovers, quickly heat remaining dressing and pour over refrigerated greens.

VEGETABLE SALADS

GERMAN POTATO SALAD

Good potato salad recipes are hard to come by, since most of the good potato salad makers operate by feel and instinct rather than by measurement. It's usually a pinch of this and a little of that. This is a recipe that has quickly become the neighborhood favorite. We're sure you'll like it, too. It keeps well in the refrigerator for several days.

SINGLE RECIPE	DOUBLE RECIPE
Yield: 3 servings	*Yield: 6 servings*
1 pound red boiling potatoes	2 pounds red boiling potatoes
2 slices bacon	4 slices bacon
2½ teaspoons flour	1 tablespoon plus 2 teaspoons flour
½ cup hot water	1 cup hot water
1½ tablespoons vinegar	1 ounce plus 1 tablespoon vinegar
2 tablespoons sugar	¼ cup sugar
½ teaspoon salt	1 teaspoon salt
Pinch pepper	Pinch pepper
½ cup chopped celery	1 cup chopped celery
¼ cup chopped green pepper, fresh or frozen	½ cup chopped green pepper, fresh or frozen
¼ cup chopped onions or green scallions, fresh or frozen	½ cup chopped onions or green scallions, fresh or frozen

Boil potatoes until done, but still firm. Cool potatoes sufficiently to be handled. Peel and slice. While the potatoes are cooking, dice bacon and fry until moderately crisp. Remove bacon from skillet or microwave oven. Add flour to the bacon grease. Blend and add hot water, vinegar, sugar, salt, and pepper, stirring constantly. When the mixture comes to a boil, lower the heat and continue simmering for several minutes. Have the chopped vegetables ready in a large mixing bowl. Add the sliced potatoes and hot potato salad dressing. Stir until well blended and set aside. German Potato Salad may be stored at room temperature, if properly covered, for several hours. Or if you prefer refrigerating overnight, it may be warmed, covered, in a low oven or microwave oven briefly before serving.

FRENCH TOMATO SALAD

This is a refreshing salad or vegetable dish that can be prepared a day in advance.

Yield: 5 servings

4 very large vine-ripened tomatoes	1 tablespoon olive oil
3 scallions, snipped	1 teaspoon vinegar
Salt and pepper to taste	Pinch basil
1 clove garlic, crushed (optional)	1 sprig parsley, snipped

Dunk tomatoes in boiling water for 1 minute. Remove from water, peel, and chop into mixing bowl. Add snipped scallions and remaining ingredients, with the exception of the parsley. Mix well and chill. Just before serving snip parsley, add to salad, and toss.

MARINATED FOUR-BEAN SALAD

This old time favorite improves as it ages. Make it several days in advance for optimum flavor.

Yield: Approximately 2 quarts

One 1-pound can cut green beans
One 1-pound can cut yellow wax
  beans
One 1-pound can garbanzo beans
One 1-pound can kidney beans
2 cups chopped celery
¾ cup green onions, snipped, stems
  and all

1 jar pimiento, chopped
½ cup chopped fresh or frozen green
  peppers
1 cup sugar
1⅓ cup vinegar
⅔ cup oil
1 teaspoon salt
Pepper to taste

Open all the cans of beans and drain thoroughly in a colander. In a large mixing bowl (preferably one with a lid) add remaining vegetables. In a saucepan combine sugar and vinegar and bring to a boil. Stir until all the sugar is dissolved. Add oil, salt, and pepper. Now add thoroughly drained beans to chopped vegetables and cover with hot marinade. Let cool at room temperature for several hours. Then refrigerate until ready to use. The minimum time salad should marinate is 24 hours.

SWEET AND SOUR ONION SALAD

This salad is marvelous to have on hand and easy to prepare; it will complement almost any meal.

Yield: Approximately 3½ cups

1 cup vinegar
⅔ cup sugar
1 teaspoon celery seed
1 green pepper, cut into julienne
  strips

1 sweet red pepper, cut into julienne
  strips
2 large Bermuda onions, sliced

Combine vinegar, sugar, and celery seed and heat until sugar is dissolved. Add all the remaining ingredients and let marinate about 4 to 5 hours. This salad keeps well in the refrigerator for several weeks.

YUMMY COLESLAW

This is a yummy dressing for coleslaw, with a slightly different twist; the horseradish sauce gives it a little bite. Keeps well in refrigerator. Great for brown baggers!

Yield: About 2 quarts coleslaw

½ cup mayonnaise
2 tablespoons Dijon-style mustard
3 tablespoons sugar
2 tablespoons cider vinegar
½ cup sour half-and-half or yogurt

2 teaspoons horseradish
1 teaspoon celery salt (optional)
1 teaspoon salt
Pepper to taste
1 medium size head cabbage

Blend all the ingredients except the cabbage and refrigerate at least 1 hour so that flavors will blend. Meanwhile, shred your cabbage and pour on the dressing. Toss until all the cabbage is evenly coated. Serve immediately or refrigerate until serving time.

Store any leftover salad in a tightly covered container in the refrigerator. Keeps well.

VEGETABLE MEDLEY SALAD

This nutritious make-ahead vegetable salad is marvelous to take on a summer picnic or to a pot-luck dinner.

Yield: 8 servings

Two 9-ounce packages frozen green
   beans
One 9-ounce package frozen
   artichoke hearts
One 6-ounce can sliced mushrooms,
   drained
¾ cup stuffed green olives, sliced
1 Bermuda onion, sliced thinly and
   separated into rings

1 clove garlic, pressed
¼ cup tarragon or wine vinegar
½ cup olive oil
1½ teaspoons salt
1 tablespoon sugar
¼ teaspoon freshly ground pepper
1 teaspoon dried salad herbs

Cook green beans and artichoke hearts according to directions on package. Drain thoroughly and cool in a large mixing bowl. Add mushrooms, olives, and onion rings. Meanwhile in a small saucepan combine garlic, vinegar, oil, salt, sugar, pepper, and herbs. Bring to a boil and simmer for 2 minutes. Pour over vegetables, toss, then chill for at least 2 hours or preferably overnight.

ORIENTAL ASPARAGUS SALAD

You'll enjoy these marinated asparagus because they're quick, different, and delicious.

Yield: 6 servings

1 to 1½ pounds fresh tender
   asparagus
1 tablespoon soy sauce

2 teaspoons toasted sesame seed oil
   or peanut oil
1 teaspoon sugar

Wash fresh asparagus and snap off tough stem ends. Line asparagus in a row on your chopping board and slice diagonally into 1-inch lengths. Drop into 2 quarts of rapidly boiling water and cook for 3 to 5 minutes until just crispy tender. Cool immediately under cold running water. Drain; lay on absorbent towels and dry completely. Combine remaining ingredients, stirring until sugar is dissolved. Put asparagus in a bowl, toss gently with dressing. Chill several hours before serving.

Don't confuse toasted sesame seed oil with European sesame oil. This oil comes from the Orient, is clear and caramel-colored, and has a very strong nutty flavor. Available in Oriental, gourmet, and specialty stores, it is a great flavoring device in many salads and vegetable dishes, as well as many Oriental dishes.

CUCUMBER SALAD

Always refreshing and pleasing to the eye. Keeps well in the refrigerator for several days.

SINGLE RECIPE	DOUBLE RECIPE
Yield: Approximately 1 to 2 cups	*Yield: Approximately 3 to 4 cups*
2 small size firm cucumbers	3 medium size firm cucumbers
2 teaspoons salt	1 tablespoon salt
½ small Spanish or Bermuda onion, sliced thin	1 small Spanish or Bermuda onion, sliced thin
½ cup sour half-and-half or yogurt	1 cup sour half-and-half or yogurt
Pepper to taste	Pepper to taste
Chives, dill, or parsley	Chives, dill, or parsley

Peel cucumbers and slice in thin slices with food processor, using slicing blade. Sprinkle with salt. Toss and let stand for 15 minutes. Squeeze out the juice. (This step removes any tart or bitter flavor in the cucumber.) Now combine cucumbers and onions with sour half-and-half or yogurt, adding freshly ground pepper, and garnish with herbs. Refrigerate until serving time.

DILLED CUCUMBER AND MACARONI SALAD

Combine your vegetables and pasta all in one. This salad goes especially well with seafood.

Yield: Approximately 5 cups

One 7 or 8-ounce package elbow
  macaroni, cooked
1 tablespoon salt
¼ cup mayonnaise
¼ cup sour half-and-half or sour
  cream
2 teaspoons lemon juice

1 tablespoon fresh chopped dill
1 teaspoon salt (or more if needed)
Dash white pepper
1 cup peeled cucumbers, cubed
2 scallions or green onions, finely
  sliced

Cook macaroni in rapidly boiling water that has been salted with 1 tablespoon of salt. Cook uncovered, stirring occasionally, until tender (usually about 7 to 8 minutes). Drain in colander and rinse with cold water. Drain again thoroughly.

In a mixing bowl combine mayonnaise, sour half-and-half, lemon juice, and seasonings, mixing well. Add macaroni, cucumbers, and green onions, and toss. Chill until serving time.

MAIN COURSE SALADS

SHRIMP SALAD

A simple and tasty entrée. Cook and refrigerate shrimp the night before.

SINGLE RECIPE
Yield: About 2 to 3 servings

½ pound cooked shrimp, shelled and
  deveined
½ cup celery, finely sliced
Lettuce (preferably several kinds),
  washed and torn
1 small size tomato, cut in wedges
1 hard-cooked egg, chopped
1 scallion, snipped, tops and all
1 sprig parsley, snipped
3 tablespoons mayonnaise
1½ teaspoons lemon juice
1½ teaspoons chili sauce
½ teaspoon horseradish
2 tablespoons piccalilli
1 clove garlic, pressed
¼ teaspoon seafood seasoning
½ teaspoon sugar
Salt and pepper to taste

DOUBLE RECIPE
Yield: About 5 to 6 servings

1 pound cooked shrimp, shelled and
  deveined
1 cup celery, finely sliced
Lettuce (preferably several kinds),
  washed and torn
1 or 2 medium size tomatoes, cut in
  wedges
2 hard-cooked eggs, chopped
2 scallions, snipped, tops and all
2 sprigs parsley, snipped
⅓ cup mayonnaise
1 tablespoon lemon juice
1 tablespoon chili sauce
1 teaspoon horseradish
¼ cup piccalilli
2 cloves garlic, pressed
½ teaspoon seafood seasoning
1 teaspoon sugar
Salt and pepper to taste

Combine shrimp, lettuce, tomatoes, eggs, onions, and parsley in a large salad bowl and toss gently. Combine the remaining ingredients in a small dish and chill until serving time. Pour over salad and toss. Serve immediately.

CURRIED HAWAIIAN CHICKEN SALAD

Serve as an elegant luncheon or a simple supper.

SINGLE RECIPE	DOUBLE RECIPE
Yield: 2 to 3 servings	*Yield: 4 to 6 servings*
1 cup cold cooked chicken, cubed	2 cups cold cooked chicken, cubed
½ cup diced celery	1 cup diced celery
One 8-ounce can unsweetened pineapple chunks, drained	One 20-ounce can unsweetened pineapple chunks, drained
2 tablespoons toasted slivered almonds	⅓ cup toasted slivered almonds
2 cups (approximately) head lettuce, washed and torn	4 cups (approximately) head lettuce, washed and torn
¼ cup mayonnaise	½ cup mayonnaise
1 teaspoon curry	2 teaspoons curry

In a large salad bowl combine chicken, celery, pineapple, nuts, and lettuce. Combine mayonnaise with curry powder, mixing well. Add to salad ingredients and toss thoroughly. Serve.

This recipe is easy to double or triple, if you need to when entertaining. If you wish to make the salad in advance, stabilize the dressing with gelatin. For a single recipe, combine 1 teaspoon unflavored gelatin with 2 tablespoons of cold water and let stand for 5 minutes. Then, in the top of a double boiler or a heat-proof custard cup set in a saucepan of boiling water, dissolve the gelatin. Remove from heat and add a little mayonnaise to the gelatin mixture; when blended, combine with mayonnaise-curry mixture.

POLYNESIAN HAM SALAD

Try this cool, refreshing meal-in-one salad, ideal for hot days when dinner preparation is best kept to a minimum and hot foods have lost their appeal. It may be made from boiled, canned, or leftover ham.

SINGLE RECIPE	DOUBLE RECIPE
Yield: 3 servings	*Yield: 6 servings*
One 8-ounce can pineapple chunks	One 13½-ounce can pineapple chunks
1½ teaspoons sugar	1 tablespoon sugar
½ teaspoon cornstarch	1 teaspoon cornstarch
1½ teaspoons lemon juice	1 tablespoon lemon juice
1 egg yolk	1 egg yolk

¼ cup sour half-and-half
1 medium size banana, cut in ½-inch slices
¼ ripe cantaloupe, cut into balls
¼ ripe honey dew melon, cut into balls
⅛ pound red cherries, pitted
⅛ pound seedless grapes, stemmed
3 tablespoons toasted coconut
½ pound cooked ham, cut into cubes

½ cup sour half-and-half
2 medium size bananas, cut in ½-inch slices
½ ripe cantaloupe, cut into balls
½ ripe honey dew melon, cut into balls
¼ pound red cherries, pitted
¼ pound seedless grapes, stemmed
⅓ cup toasted coconut
1 pound cooked ham, cut into cubes

Drain pineapple chunks, reserving the juice. In a saucepan combine sugar and cornstarch. Add ¼ cup of pineapple juice, lemon juice, and egg yolk. Cook over medium heat, stirring constantly until thickened. Cool slightly, then fold in sour half-and-half. Chill. (This part can be made ahead.)

Meanwhile, combine drained pineapple chunks, banana slices (which have been dipped in remaining pineapple juice to prevent discoloring), remaining fruits, coconut, and ham. Toss lightly and chill until ready to serve. Just before serving combine chilled dressing with fruit-ham mixture and toss. Serve on a lettuce bed.

MEXICAN CHEF SALAD

This salad is a meal in itself. The recipe might look complicated, but it is really quite simple.

SINGLE RECIPE
   Yield: 3 to 4 servings (as an entrée)

½ pound lean ground beef
One 8-ounce can kidney beans, drained
¼ teaspoon salt
½ teaspoon cumin
Chili or hot sauce to taste
2 green onions, snipped
2 medium ripe tomatoes, chopped
¼ large head of lettuce
2 ounces shredded Cheddar cheese
1 rounded tablespoon sliced ripe olives
½ avocado
1½ teaspoons lemon juice
Thousand Island or French dressing
½ cup corn chips (plain or taco-flavored)

DOUBLE RECIPE
   Yield: 6 to 8 servings (as an entrée)

1 pound lean ground beef
One 15-ounce can kidney beans, drained
½ teaspoon salt
1 teaspoon cumin
Chili or hot sauce to taste
4 green onions, snipped
4 medium ripe tomatoes, chopped
½ large head of lettuce
4 ounces shredded Cheddar cheese
One 2¼-ounce can sliced ripe olives
1 avocado
1 tablespoon lemon juice
Thousand Island or French dressing
Approximately 1 cup corn chips (plain or taco-flavored)

Brown meat in a large skillet, draining off any fat. Add drained kidney beans and seasonings, and continue cooking for 5 minutes over low heat.

Meanwhile, in a large salad bowl combine the following ingredients: snipped onions, chopped tomatoes, shredded lettuce, grated cheese, and olives. Toss lightly. Peel, halve, and slice avocado. Cover with lemon juice and toss lightly. Add meat and bean combination to salad. Add dressing. Toss again ever so gently. Add corn chips and avocado pieces, toss, and serve immediately. Or you may wish to serve it plain and let each individual use the dressing of his or her choice.

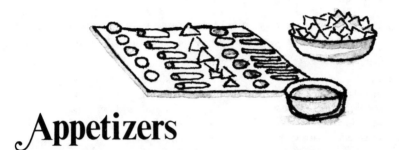

Appetizers

Although appetizers are traditionally served before a meal, with the intent of stimulating your appetite, appetizers have become such a favorite American food that we now serve them at other times. In Hawaii they're called pupus, and are served at any time or occasion when friends gather. I think that is the way we all should treat these delectable little tidbits.

Many appetizers and hors d'oeuvres can be made ahead and frozen. Others are served in chafing dishes for the guests to help themselves, and yet others are put under the broiler and heated briefly before serving. Included in this chapter are a variety of simple hors d'oeuvres and appetizers. Have you ever tried making an entire buffet meal out of these delicacies? Your guests will absolutely adore it!

Old Standbys

You may have forgotten some of these: Cubes of sharp Cheddar cheese topped with a stuffed olive on a toothpick.

Cheese and crackers, and sausage with a variety of party breads.

Cream cheese and caviar with crackers.

Smoked oysters.

A prepared frozen pizza, baked according to instructions and cut into small squares.

Hot dog slices topped with dill pickle sliced, and cubes of Cheddar or American cheese on a toothpick.

Quick dips from (1) a pint of sour cream and a package of onion soup mix (calorie-counters may prefer half yogurt and half sour half-and-half) and served with chips; (2) a pint of sour half-and-half mixed with a package of vegetable soup mix, refrigerated for several hours, and served with fresh vegetables

ANTIPASTO

Arrange on a large tray, nicely decorated with greens, a selection of the following. Use as many as you wish in a quantity suitable to the number of persons you are serving.

Italian cheeses, such as
   mozzarella, provolone,
   Gorgonzola, or Bel Paese
Green and ripe olives
Anchovies rolled with capers
Marinated mushrooms (see below)
Solid-pack tuna, in bite-size pieces
Green onions
Salami, pepperoni, or prosciutto,
   sliced thin and rolled
Cherry tomatoes
Hot and mild peppers
Artichoke hearts
Pimientos
Radishes
Bread sticks
Shrimp

Serve antipasto with an ample supply of picks, together with a nice dry Italian wine and garlic bread, if you wish. When serving a large group, I like to cover a Styrofoam cone with endive and other greens. Then cover with cheese squares, olives, anchovies, marinated mushrooms, and shrimp, all attached with toothpicks or spears. Set in center of large platter and surround with remaining ingredients. Makes a most impressive picture. Remember, there's no cooking and it's fun to arrange.

MARINATED MUSHROOMS

Once you make these, you'll never want to be without them. Covered, they keep in the refrigerator for months. (I've never been that lucky; mine always disappear.) They are particularly marvelous as an appetizer but can also be served as an accompaniment to any meat, especially steaks. They take only a few minutes to prepare.

Yield: Approximately 2½ cups

1 pound mushrooms
3 teaspoons salt
1 cup olive oil
4 cloves garlic, minced
½ cup vinegar
About 6 drops onion juice
Finely chopped fresh herbs
   (optional)

Select only very fresh, firm mushrooms. The best are the large fat ones with short stems. Do not select mushrooms with flat tops and dark gills showing beneath, as they discolor. Soak mushrooms in cold water for 5 minutes to loosen any soil. Put them into a plastic bag and fill it with sufficient water to generously cover the mushrooms. Hold the bag closed with one hand and agitate vigorously with the other. Drain in colander. If they are not completely clean, repeat. Trim stem ends if needed and place mushrooms in a large heavy skillet (no shortening is needed). Sprinkle salt over the mushrooms and simmer, covered, over moderate heat for 15 minutes. Remove from heat and drain. Meanwhile, mix the remaining ingredients and pour into the glass container in which you are going to store your mushrooms. Add warm mushrooms, cover, and allow them to marinate at room temperature overnight. Stir occasionally and refrigerate.

These mushrooms are especially delicious in a tossed salad. Slice mushrooms in half if they are large and toss a generous amount in your salad. Serve with vinegar and oil dressing.

VARIATION. Use the same marinade and the same procedure with frozen artichoke hearts, green pepper squares, or any other vegetable.

APPETIZERS BY THE YARD

To make appetizers by the yard, buy an 18-inch loaf of sandwich or butter-crust bread at your local bakery and have it sliced the long way rather than the traditional way. Toast one side of these long bread slices under the oven broiler on cookie sheets, watching closely so they don't burn. Now spread the untoasted side with any type of spread that tastes good broiled or baked. Return to cookie sheet and bake or broil according to instructions; then cut into squares, sticks, or triangles and serve.

These can be made a day ahead and be refrigerated or frozen. Freeze on cookie sheets for about 1 hour. Insert a double thickness of waxed paper between the slices of bread and stack. Wrap in heavy duty foil or large freezer bags, label, date, and freeze. Wrap each variety of filling in a separate package to avoid transfer of flavors.

TO SERVE WHEN FROZEN. Simply remove the number of slices you wish to use, being careful to rewrap the package securely before returning it to the freezer. Put long slices of bread on a cookie sheet and let them thaw for 30 minutes. Place under the broiler until topping is heated through and a bit bubbly. Now cut slices into triangles, squares, or strips and arrange them on a serving plate or platter. Garnishes that are easy yet very attractive include, sliced or halved ripe or green stuffed olives, sliced hard-boiled eggs, anchovies rolled with capers, caviar, and anything else that strikes your fancy. For more ideas see the following recipes.

CHEESE AND OLIVE SPREAD

These usually disappear rather quickly.

*Yield: Filling for 3 long slices of
   sandwich loaf bread, or
   approximately 36 appetizers*

8 ounces Cheddar cheese, shredded
   or ground
½ cup green onions, sliced fine
One 2¼-ounce can sliced ripe olives,
   drained
One 2-ounce jar pimientos, drained
   and chopped

2 teaspoons Dijon mustard
1 teaspoon salt
2 tablespoons sour cream or sour
   half-and-half
2 tablespoons mayonnaise

Combine all the ingredients in a mixing bowl. If you are using a food processor, grate the cheese and slice the olives with the grating and slicing blades. Then put on the plastic mixing blade and mix the remaining ingredients, being careful not to overmix. Follow instructions for making Appetizers by the Yard.

Garnish with partially cooked bacon before broiling or fully cooked crumbled bacon after broiling. Small or halved shrimp also make good garnishes.

SWISS CRAB APPETIZER SPREAD

Really yummy!

*Yield: Filling for 2 long slices of
   sandwich loaf bread*

One 7½-ounce can crab meat,
   drained and flaked, or one 8-ounce
   package frozen crab meat
1 cup grated Swiss cheese
   (approximately 4 ounces)
2 tablespoons mayonnaise
2 tablespoons sour cream or sour
   half-and-half

1 tablespoon lemon juice
½ teaspoon salt
Pepper to taste
½ teaspoon curry powder, hot or
   mild
Sliced black olives or pimientos
   (optional)

Combine all the ingredients. Prepare as described under Appetizers by the Yard (page 143). Just before serving, place bread slices on a large cookie sheet under the broiler for a few minutes until bubbly and lightly browned. (Watch carefully, as they burn easily.) Cut into squares, triangles, or oblong strips. Garnish with olive slices or pimiento strips if you wish. Serve immediately.

When frozen, allow bread slices to thaw for about ½ hour before placing under broiler.

QUICKIE SHRIMP PUFFS

These delectable canapes can be made in just a minute's time. Keep this recipe in mind, as it can be a real lifesaver in an emergency. It's made with ingredients that you can always have on hand.

Yield: Approximately 2 dozen
small canapes

White bread
One 7½-ounce can shrimp
1 cup mayonnaise

½ cup shredded sharp Cheddar
    cheese

Toast bread on one side under broiler. (Or take two slices from a sandwich loaf of bread cut horizontally and use this as your base.) Sprinkle drained shrimp evenly on white bread. Combine the mayonnaise with the Cheddar cheese and spread over shrimp, covering the bread entirely. Just before serving, insert under the broiler at 350°F for about 3 minutes, or until mixture is hot and slightly browning. Cut bread into various shapes, such as squares, oblong fingers, or triangles.

DIPS

SPINACH DIP

Not only is it delicious, but also the lovely green color is a welcome addition.

Yield: Approximately 3 cups

One 10-ounce package frozen
    chopped spinach, thawed
½ cup chopped fresh parsley
½ cup green onions, coarsely
    chopped
½ teaspoon dill weed

½ teaspoon seasoned salt
1 cup mayonnaise
1 cup sour cream or sour
    half-and-half
½ teaspoon oregano
Juice of ½ lemon (1½ tablespoons)

Put all the ingredients in your blender and blend until smooth. Refrigerate at least 12 hours before serving. Very good with assorted fresh vegetables.

CLAM DIP

Always be sure to have ingredients for this on your pantry shelf. It can be a real lifesaver.

Yield: Approximately 1½ cups

1 cup sour cream or sour
  half-and-half
One 7½-ounce can minced clams,
  drained
1 teaspoon onion salt

½ teaspoon garlic salt
2 teaspoons Worcestershire sauce
1 teaspoon lemon juice
Dash salt
Few drops Tabasco sauce (to taste)

Combine all the above ingredients and serve, or refrigerate until serving time. Serve with potato chips or corn chips. It is especially good served with fresh vegetables.

CHEESE APPETIZERS

CURRIED CHEESE BALLS

This is the type of recipe in which the ingredients don't sound as good as they really taste.

SINGLE RECIPE

One 8-ounce package Cheddar
  cheese
One 8-ounce package cream cheese
1 teaspoon curry powder (more if
  desired)

1 tablespoon sherry wine
Chopped green onions
Chutney

Grate Cheddar cheese. Mix cream cheese until soft and creamy, adding curry powder and sherry wine. Add grated Cheddar cheese and mix until well blended, or use a food processor for the entire operation. Form into 2 or 3 small balls. This will eliminate having a half-eaten cheese ball left over. Before serving, cover with chopped nut meats, and garnish with chopped green onions and chutney. When well wrapped, cheese balls will keep in the refrigerator for several weeks.

CHEESE SNACKS

Really a nifty appetizer made just like cookies, these cheese snacks make a quick treat you'll enjoy serving.

Yield: About 75 appetizers

1 cup butter or margarine (2 sticks)
½ pound Cheddar cheese
1 teaspoon salt

2 cups flour
2 cups Rice Krispies

Preheat oven to 350°F. Cream butter. Shred cheese and add to butter along with salt and flour. (Use the grating blade of your food processor if you have one; then mix cheese with flour using metal blade.) When the mixture is well blended, gently fold in the Rice Krispies. Roll the dough on waxed paper into a long rope, about ¾ inch in diameter. Wrap and refrigerate until baking time. Cut into ⅜-inch thick slices. Place on an ungreased cookie sheet. With a fork, flatten each piece of dough, making an indentation on each snack with the fork prongs. Bake at 350°F for 18 to 20 minutes. Watch carefully, as they burn easily. Remove from oven when just nicely browned.

VARIATION. Add ¼ teaspoon cayenne pepper or ½ teaspoon oregano or both when you cream the butter.

TO FREEZE. Freezer-wrap the roll of unbaked dough, date, label, and freeze.

TO SERVE WHEN FROZEN. Remove dough from freezer and thaw at room temperature for about 30 minutes. Slice and bake according to above instructions.

APPETIZERS OF MEAT, SEAFOOD, OR POULTRY

SAUSAGE BALLS

Made just like cookies, sausage balls are a quickie appetizer you'll always want on hand. Great served with soup, too. They freeze well.

Yield: About 100 appetizers

½ pound mild pork sausage
½ pound hot pork sausage
1 pound sharp Cheddar cheese, grated

3 cups biscuit mix

In your mixing bowl combine the uncooked pork sausage with the cheese until well blended. Add biscuit mix and mix thoroughly. (A half recipe can be made in seconds with your food processor. First grate cheese, using grating blade. Then use steel blade for mixing.) Bake in a preheated 375°F oven for 10 minutes, or until nicely browned. Keep warm while serving on a hot tray.

TO FREEZE. Freeze balls before baking. Place on large cookie sheet and freeze. When frozen, remove from cookie sheet, freezer-wrap, date, label, and return to freezer.

TO SERVE WHEN FROZEN. Thaw and bake according to above instructions.

VARIATIONS. All hot pork sausage may be used, but the balls will definitely be quite spicy. Do not use all mild sausage, as this gives them a very bland flavor. If you can't find the hot sausage, add ¼ teaspoon of cayenne pepper, or more if you like, to a single recipe.

WATER CHESTNUTS WRAPPED IN BACON

Don't forget this old standby! It can also be made with chicken livers (see Variation).

Yield: Approximately 24 to 36,
   depending on size of water
   chestnuts

½ pound bacon   Brown sugar
Soy sauce   Two 6-ounce cans water chestnuts

Preheat oven to 400°F. Cut bacon strips in half and lay flat in a single layer on broiling pan. Sprinkle with soy sauce and brown sugar. Put bacon into oven for about 15 to 20 minutes, watching closely at end of baking time (or cook in your microwave oven). Bacon should be almost done but not crisp. Remove bacon from broiling pan and drain on absorbent paper. Now wrap one half slice of bacon around each water chestnut (if large), securing each with a toothpick. Use ⅓ slice bacon for each small chestnut. Return to oven for another 5 minutes or until bacon is very crispy.

TO FREEZE. Do not return bacon-wrapped water chestnuts to oven. Place on oven-proof platter or dish. Freeze, wrap, date and label.

TO SERVE WHEN FROZEN. Either thaw at room temperature and bake according to directions, or bake frozen for approximately 10 to 15 minutes. Watch closely toward end of baking time.

VARIATION. Substitute chicken livers for water chestnuts. Sauté chicken livers for 5 minutes in butter while bacon is in the oven. Follow preceding instructions.

BACON WANDS

Here is another quickie.

Yield: 24 appetizers
12 slices bacon
12 thin salted bread sticks

Preheat oven to 400°F. Wrap bacon in spiral fashion around bread sticks. Arrange on a broiler pan with ends of bacon on underside of bread sticks. Bake at 400°F for about 15 minutes or until bacon is crisply cooked. Cut in half and serve warm.

BEEF TARTARE

Served with a fresh tomato salad (see page 133), this makes a wonderful lunch or supper. Serve with fresh thin-sliced rye bread.

SINGLE RECIPE
  Yield: 6–8 servings as an appetizer

1 pound round sirloin tip steak, ground
2 green onions, chopped finely, stems and all
2 egg yolks
½ teaspoon salt
Dash freshly ground pepper
Thin-sliced cocktail rye rounds

DOUBLE RECIPE
  Yield: 12–16 servings as an appetizer

2 pounds round sirloin tip steak, ground
4 green onions, chopped finely, stems and all
3 egg yolks
1 teaspoon salt
⅛ teaspoon freshly ground pepper
Thin-sliced cocktail rye rounds

From a 2-pound piece of round sirloin tip steak have your butcher trim all the fat and bone, then grind it twice. Or do it yourself using a food processor or meat grinder.

In a large mixing bowl combine meat, onions, egg yolks, salt, and pepper. Mix until all the ingredients are well combined. Beef Tartare can be served in small balls on top of crackers or toasted rye rounds. It is quicker and easier, though, to serve Beef Tartare mounded in the center of a platter, surrounded by an assortment of toasted cocktail rye rounds and crackers.

To toast cocktail rye, butter lightly (optional) and place on a cookie sheet. Put under broiler until just barely brown, then turn. Serve warm. Arrange around tartare balls and serve.

TO SERVE AS AN ENTRÉE. Shape into individual patties or 1 large mound on a serving platter. Garnish with snipped parsley. Serve with fresh or toasted rye bread, French or Italian bread, or hard rolls.

VARIATION. Small pieces of anchovy or capers may be pressed on top of some of the tartare balls, adding more variations.

HAM ROLLS

Sure to be a hit, these picture-pretty ham rolls are as good served as an appetizer as on a cold meat and cheese platter.

  Yield: 24 ham rolls

One 3-ounce package cream cheese
1 teaspoon chopped onion
2 teaspoons horseradish
½ teaspoon dry mustard

12 thin slices cooked lean ham
Mayonnaise
Parsley, finely snipped

Have cream cheese at room temperature. With electric mixer or food processor blend chopped onions, horseradish, and mustard with the cream cheese. Cover each slice of ham with a thin layer of the cheese mixture, using up all of it. Roll up each piece of ham in a jelly-roll fashion and secure with toothpicks. Cut each ham roll in half. Dip end of roll in mayonnaise and then in finely snipped parsley; arrange on platter. Cover with plastic wrap and refrigerate until serving time.

ORIENTAL CHICKEN WINGS

Inexpensive, delicious, easy, and sure to be a favorite.

Yield: Approximately 40 to 50
pieces

4 green onions and tops, thinly
   sliced
1 cup soy sauce
1 cup sherry wine
1 cup water
¼ cup honey
¼ cup brown sugar

1 clove garlic, pressed
1 teaspoon powdered ginger
½ teaspoon cinnamon
Pinch ground cloves
3 pounds plump chicken wings
   (approximately 20 to 25)

In a large heavy skillet mix onions, soy sauce, sherry, water, honey, brown sugar, garlic, and spices. Cook until boiling. Meanwhile, wash chicken wings. Cut off the wing tips (save these for chicken stock). With a sharp knife disjoint wings or ask your butcher to do this. Add to sauce and simmer for about 40 minutes, or until chicken wings are well browned and coated. Turn chicken wings frequently, particularly if you are making a large batch. It is not necessary to brown the wings beforehand; the sauce browns the chicken wings to a delectable color.

Serve with slotted spoon in chafing dish, electric skillet, or buffet server.

BROILED SCAMPI IN GARLIC BUTTER

For something different from the usual shrimp and cocktail sauce, try this quickie! Use it as an appetizer or an entrée.

Yield: 6 servings as an entrée,
more as an appetizer

2 pounds unpeeled shrimp, or 1½
   pounds peeled and deveined
   frozen shrimp
¼ pound (1 stick) butter

1 large clove garlic, pressed
Salt and pepper to taste
Parsley

Remove shells from shrimp, cut down center of back, and remove sand vein. Melt butter in a small saucepan, add pressed garlic, and simmer for about 3 minutes over moderate heat. Place shrimp in a large oven-to-table serving dish or platter. Pour garlic butter over shrimp and toss until all the shrimp are covered. Sprinkle with salt and pepper. Place in preheated broiler and broil for about 5 to 7 minutes, or until the shrimp are tender, tossing the shrimp once. Garnish with parsley and serve immediately.

VARIATION. To make this entrée, add a 10-ounce package of frozen mixed Chinese vegetables that have been thawed. Add when tossing the shrimp, midway during baking period. Add soy sauce, if desired.

HERRING ANTIPASTO

A marvelous appetizer or first course. Keeps well in the refrigerator for several weeks (that is, if you can stop noshing).

Yield: Approximately 5 cups

One 2-pound jar herring in wine sauce

½ red onion, chopped

1 green pepper, chopped

1 jar of marinated artichokes, drained and sliced

One 12-ounce bottle Bennett's chili sauce

Two 2¼-ounce cans sliced olives, or one 6-ounce can pitted olives, sliced

Drain herring and cut into strips. Dice onion. In large mixing bowl add chopped pepper and sliced artichoke hearts, together with all the other ingredients. (Frozen artichoke hearts cooked according to package directions may be substituted for the marinated ones.) Mix well and marinate in refrigerator about 6 hours before serving.

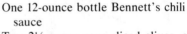

Desserts

Does the word "dessert" conjure up in your mind visions of cakes with delectable frosting, homemade pies a la mode and cream-filled pastries? While the aforementioned desserts are extraordinarily good, they are usually too rich and calorie-laden for everyday eating; they also usually involve quite a bit of time in preparation or are terribly expensive to purchase.

A simple dessert, such as fruit and cheese, is a delicious and satisfying way of ending a meal. Pears with Brie or Bel Paese, apples with Cheddar or Colby cheese, or grapes with Monterey Jack or Gouda are some of my favorites.

A dish of fresh blueberries topped with peaches, a dab of sour cream, and a bit of real maple syrup is pure ecstasy (see page 158). (It's also great for breakfast.)

Fresh peaches topped with raspberry liqueur or a fresh fruit compote made with blueberries, strawberries, bananas, and fresh or canned unsweetened pineapple is delectable. You can keep the leftovers in the refrigerator for another day or two. Prepare this for Sunday brunch and have the leftovers for dessert on Monday or Tuesday.

Much can be done with frozen yogurt and ice cream. They can be used to make a small banana split topped with fresh roasted nuts or coconut and topped with chocolate sauce (see page 171). A flavored liqueur served over frozen yogurt or ice cream makes a truly elegant dessert. Besides the famous crème de menthe served over ice cream balls at all banquet halls, there are many other interesting combinations. Use coffee or chocolate ice cream topped with coffee-flavored liqueur, such as Kahlua or Tia Maria. Any other fruit-flavored liqueur is equally delicious over vanilla or fruit-flavored ice cream with or without fresh fruit. For example, use French vanilla or peach ripple ice cream topped with fresh peaches, and then spoon peach brandy and almonds over the top.

You are only limited by your own imagination; the variations are endless.

BLENDER DESSERTS

The following blender-made (or food processor) desserts take only a minimum amount of time. For a quickie dessert, pour them into parfait glasses and refrigerate until serving time. For a more elaborate dessert, pour into a prepared pie shell or crumb crust. One of these fillings can also be made into a torte by putting a crust in the bottom of a 9-inch spring form pan. This makes a most elegant dessert, ideal when entertaining.

When you use a food processor, put the solid foods in first; for example, put the ice cream in the work bowl, put on the lid, and activate the food processor. Then pour the liquid through the feed tube. Do just the opposite when you work with a blender.

When making frozen desserts and parfaits in individual parfait glasses, set your stemware in a 6- or 8-pack soft drink carton. Not only will this keep your stemware upright, but also it will protect it from breakage. Removing the glassware from the freezer is also simplified.

BLENDER BAVARIAN CREAM

This marvelous dessert can be made in your blender in less than 5 minutes and takes only 10 minutes to "ripen." It's a great recipe when time is precious. The recipe makes a 9-inch torte or a 10-inch pie with crumb crust.

Vanilla Bavarian Cream

Yield: 6 to 8 servings

½ cup cold milk	¼ cup sugar
2 envelopes unflavored gelatin	1 to 2 teaspoons vanilla extract
¾ cup milk, heated to boiling	1 cup whipping cream
2 eggs	1¼ cups crushed ice or ice cubes

Put cold milk in your blender and add gelatin. Let stand for 3 minutes. Stir at low speed; add boiling milk slowly. If gelatin granules cling to container use, a spatula to push them down into liquid. When the gelatin is dissolved add eggs, sugar, and extract. (Have the blender going on low speed all this time.) Cover and turn to high speed. Add cream through feeder cap. When well blended, add ice and continue blending until all the ice is liquefied. Pour into individual serving dishes or a 5-cup mold. Chill until serving time.

CAUTION. Have serving dishes handy, because after the ice has been liquefied, the gelatin mixture sets rather quickly.

For a fluffier texture, whip cream separately and fold into gelatin mixture.

VARIATIONS. Reduce vanilla extract to 1 teaspoon and add 2 tablespoons of coffee liqueur, fruit cordial, or brandy. Two tablespoons of instant coffee may also be added to the boiling milk.

Crème de Menthe Bavarian

Prepare Vanilla Bavarian Cream as directed and add 3 to 4 tablespoons of crème de menthe to mixture before adding whipping cream.

Chocolate Bavarian

After adding the boiling milk, add 1 cup of semisweet chocolate morsels and continue blending until all the chocolate is melted.

STRAWBERRY BAVARIAN CREAM

This dessert is particularly attractive when garnished with fresh strawberries.

Yield: One 5-cup mold

One 16-ounce package frozen strawberries, partially thawed	2 eggs, separated
2 envelopes unflavored gelatin	1 cup whipping cream
½ cup milk, heated to boiling	¾ cup crushed ice or ice cubes

Thaw strawberries sufficiently to drain ½ cup of cold juice from them. Put juice in blender and add gelatin. Mix on low speed until all the gelatin has been moistened. Add boiling milk and continue blending until gelatin is dissolved. Add egg yolks, one at a time. Now add whipping cream and turn speed to high, just briefly. Stop blender. Add strawberries and remaining juice. Turn blender on high, add ice, and continue processing until ice is liquefied. Beat egg whites until stiff and fold into strawberry mixture. Pour immediately into individual serving dishes or a 5-cup mold. Refrigerate until firm, at least 3 or 4 hours for a mold.

COFFEE SOUFFLÉ

This elegant offering can be made as a low-carbohydrate dessert, as well as a regular dessert, depending on whether you use sweeteners or sugar in the ingredients.

SINGLE RECIPE
Yield: 4 to 5 servings

1 package (1 tablespoon) unflavored gelatin
2 tablespoons cold water
1½ teaspoons instant freeze-dried coffee
1 cup water
¾ cup whipping cream
⅓ cup sugar or equivalent sweetener
Dash salt

DOUBLE RECIPE
Yield: 8 to 10 servings

2 packages (2 tablespoons) unflavored gelatin
¼ cup cold water
1 tablespoon instant freeze-dried coffee
2 cups water
1½ cups whipping cream
⅔ cups sugar or equivalent sweetener
Pinch salt

Soak gelatin in cold water for 3 minutes, then place over low heat or boiling water until all the gelatin granules have been dissolved (about 5 seconds in your microwave oven). Mix freeze-dried coffee with water, stirring until all the granules are dissolved. Add to gelatin mixture and chill until slightly thickened. Whip whipping cream, add sugar or sweetener and salt, and fold into gelatin mixture. Pour into one of your prettiest 4-cup molds and refrigerate for several hours. Unmold to serve.

VARIATION. For Mocha soufflé add one tablespoon of cocoa with the instant coffee. You may have to heat the water a bit to dissolve the cocoa. Also, sugar or sweetener will have to be increased.

GRASSHOPPER ICE

This blender dessert is made with chocolate ice cream, crème de cacao, and crème de menthe. Serve it in sherbet or parfait glasses, much as you would Brandied Ice.

SINGLE RECIPE
Yield: Three 4-ounce servings

1 ounce (2 tablespoons) white crème de menthe
1 ounce (2 tablespoons) crème de cacao
1 pint chocolate ice cream

DOUBLE RECIPE
Yield: Six 4-ounce servings

2 ounces (¼ cup) white crème de menthe
2 ounces (¼ cup) crème de cacao
1 quart chocolate ice cream

Pour liqueur into blender; add ice cream a scoop or two at a time, blending until smooth after each addition. When you use a food processor, reverse the procedure and put the ice cream in the work bowl first, then add liqueurs. Pour into sherbet or parfait glasses and serve immediately. Dessert may be garnished with chocolate curls or a fresh sprig of mint.

POTS DE CRÈME

So easy to make in your blender.

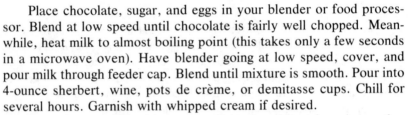

Yield: 6 servings

One 6-ounce package semisweet chocolate pieces	½ cup sugar
	3 eggs
1 ounce unsweetened chocolate	1 cup milk

Place chocolate, sugar, and eggs in your blender or food processor. Blend at low speed until chocolate is fairly well chopped. Meanwhile, heat milk to almost boiling point (this takes only a few seconds in a microwave oven). Have blender going at low speed, cover, and pour milk through feeder cap. Blend until mixture is smooth. Pour into 4-ounce sherbert, wine, pots de crème, or demitasse cups. Chill for several hours. Garnish with whipped cream if desired.

VARIATION. Add 2 tablespoons of brandy, white crème de menthe, crème de cacao, Grande Marnier, Kahlua, Tia Maria, Sabra, Chocolate Almond Liqueur, or any other flavor that would go well with chocolate.

FIVE-MINUTE SHERRY CREAM FREEZE

Want to serve something different, although you feel you don't have time to prepare it? Try this recipe. The delightful part of this quick dessert is that it can be made in advance and frozen.

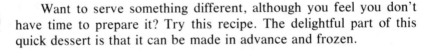

Yield: 4 to 5 servings

⅓ cup sugar	3 egg yolks
2 tablespoons water	1 pint whipping cream
2 tablespoons cream sherry wine	¼ cup toasted slivered almonds

Combine sugar and water in a small saucepan and boil rapidly for 3 minutes until sugar is dissolved and mixture is clear. In your blender or food processor, combine cream sherry and egg yolks, mixing well. Gradually pour hot syrup in a steady stream through feeder tube or cap into the egg yolk mixture while blending.

Whip cream until quite stiff. Gently fold egg yolk mixture into whipped cream. Spoon into sherbet glasses, custard cups, or paper or china soufflé cups. Sprinkle with toasted slivered almonds; set on a tray in your freezer and freeze until firm. If you are not going to serve this dessert immediately, cover the tops of the sherbet glasses or cups with clear plastic wrap or foil for longer freezer storage.

TO SERVE. Remove from freezer about 10 minutes before serving.

FRUIT DESSERTS

CHOCOLATE CHERI-SUISSE JUBILEE

Easier than Cherries Jubilee, this Chocolate-Cherry dessert is a dream.

Yield: 3 cups

One 16-ounce can pitted dark sweet cherries in heavy syrup
1 cup hot fudge sauce, purchased or homemade

¾ cup Cheri-Suisse liqueur
¼ cup brandy or rum
French Vanilla ice cream

Drain cherries and pour syrup into flambé pan or skillet. Add Hot Fudge Sauce and ½ cup Cheri-Suisse liqueur. Heat entire mixture until hot and slightly bubbly. Add cherries, stirring to mix well. Then add the last ¼ cup of the Cheri-Suisse, combined with the brandy or rum, and pour into a large gravy ladle that is resting in the center of the pan. Let the Cheri-Suisse, brandy, or rum mixture run over the top of the gravy ladle into the melted chocolate mixture. (This will keep the liqueur from mixing; it will lie on top of the chocolate mixture.) Then ignite; let the flame burn out or blow it out so that some of the alcohol remains. Spoon over French vanilla ice cream and serve.

TROPICAL PINEAPPLE FLAMBÉ

A real quickie and so good!

Yield: About 6 servings

One 8-ounce can crushed pineapple
2 tablespoons butter
⅔ cup Kahlua

⅓ cup rum
Chocolate ice cream

Drain pineapple, reserving juice. Sauté pineapple in butter for a few minutes. Add pineapple juice and Kahlua. Continue cooking until warmed. Carefully pour rum into a gravy ladle held in the center of the pineapple sauce and let the rum float on top of the mixture. Let the rum heat for a few minutes and then ignite; stir and serve over chocolate ice cream.

VARIATION. Add 1 or 2 ripe but firm bananas to pineapple mixture and sauté together. Then continue with recipe as above.

SABRA FLAMBÉ

This impressive, yet simple, dessert will be especially appreciated by all your chocolate-loving friends. Sabra is a chocolate-orange liqueur from Israel.

Yield: 2 cups

Two 3-ounce bars Toblerone chocolate-orange	½ cup Sabra
½ cup hot fudge sauce, purchased or homemade	¼ cup Sabra
	¼ cup brandy
	Grated rind of one orange (optional)

In a flambé pan or a small skillet on your stove, melt chocolate, hot fudge sauce, and ½ cup of Sabra over very low heat, stirring until the chocolate is melted smooth and the mixture is reasonably warm and bubbly. Pour remaining ¼ cup of Sabra, mixed with brandy, into a large ladle that is resting in the center of the pan. Let the Sabra run over the top of the gravy ladle onto the chocolate Sabra mixture. (This will keep the liqueur from mixing; it will lie on top of the chocolate mixture.) Wait for a half-minute so that the Sabra-brandy mixture becomes warm. Then ignite; let flame burn out, or blow it out so that some of the alcohol remains. Spoon over ice cream and serve. Ice cream flavors that complement Sabra Flambé are vanilla, chocolate, and orange sherbet.

SPARKLING STRAWBERRIES

Try these Sparkling Strawberries made with Pink Chablis, a delicious, all round sparkling sweet wine whose good flavor belies its cost. Use remaining wine to serve with your dinner.

Yield: 6 to 8 servings

1 quart strawberries	2 teaspoons Cointreau
⅓ cup sugar (or to taste)	2 teaspoons brandy
2 teaspoons kirsch	¾ cup Pink Chablis

Wash and hull strawberries. Slice large strawberries in half. Sprinkle with sugar and chill. Approximately one-half hour before serving, add liqueurs and return to refrigerator. Add wine at serving time. Spoon into attractive glasses or dishes.

BLUEBERRY PEACHES A LA CRÈME

This delightful treat can be served as a fruit compote for brunch or as a dessert. It is really simple to prepare, but the flavor combination is something you'll long remember.

Yield: 6 cups

1 pint fresh blueberries
3 cups sliced peaches

½ cup sour half-and-half or yogurt
¼ to ½ cup maple syrup

Blueberries should be washed and thoroughly dried. Dip peaches in scalding water, peel, and slice. Combine in a large mixing bowl with remaining ingredients. Toss gently. Add just enough maple syrup to give mixture a pleasantly sweet flavor. (The amount will vary, depending on the sweetness of the peaches and blueberries.) Fruit should be served at room temperature.

VARIATION. Try omitting the peaches and using 2 pints of blueberries. A great breakfast treat.

PUDDINGS

APPLESAUCE BREAD PUDDING

This is truly an outstanding bread pudding. Serve warm with cream or ice cream. Great for using stale bread.

SINGLE RECIPE
Yield: 4 servings

Approximately 6 slices white bread or an equivalent amount of French bread, sliced in ½-inch slices
2 eggs
½ cup sugar
½ teaspoon cinnamon
⅛ teaspoon nutmeg
⅛ teaspoon mace
¼ teaspoon salt
1 teaspoon vanilla
1½ cups milk
1 tablespoon butter or margarine, melted
One 8-ounce jar or can applesauce
¼ cup raisins (optional)

DOUBLE RECIPE
Yield: About 8 servings

Approximately 12 slices white bread or an equivalent amount of French bread, sliced in ½-inch slices
4 eggs
1 cup sugar
1 teaspoon cinnamon
¼ teaspoon nutmeg
¼ teaspoon mace
½ teaspoon salt
2 teaspoons vanilla
3 cups milk
2 tablespoons butter or margarine, melted
One 16-ounce jar or can applesauce
½ cup raisins (optional)

Preheat oven to 325°F. Arrange half of bread to cover the bottom of an 11 × 7 × 2-inch baking dish (for double recipe; use a 1-quart baking dish for single recipe). If you wish, sprinkle half the raisins over the bread. In your blender or food processor, combine eggs, sugar, spices, salt, vanilla, milk, and melted butter. In a large mixing bowl combine applesauce with blended ingredients, mixing well. Pour half the mixture over the bread (add optional raisins) in the baking dish. Repeat with another layer of bread, then pour remaining applesauce-milk mixture over bread. Bake at 325°F for 1 hour, or until custard is set and bread is lightly browned. This pudding is best served warm.

CHOCOLATE RICE PUDDING

This is a chocolate variation of an old favorite, spiced with rum flavoring. A great way to use leftover rice.

*Yield: 1½ quarts, or
    approximately 3 servings*

1½ cups cooked rice
1½ cups milk
⅓ cup sugar
¼ teaspoon salt
¼ teaspoon cinnamon

Pinch nutmeg
One 6-ounce package (1 cup)
    semisweet chocolate pieces
2 eggs, separated
1 teaspoon rum flavoring

In a large sauce pan combine rice with ½ cup milk and sugar. Add salt and spices. Cook until boiling, stirring constantly. Remove from heat and stir in chocolate pieces. In mixing bowl or blender combine egg yolks with remaining milk and rum flavoring. Add to chocolate rice mixture. Beat egg whites until stiff and fold into chocolate rice. Pour into a buttered 1½-quart casserole and bake at 325°F for approximately 55 minutes. The pudding will still be moist when it is removed from the oven. It may be served either warm or cold.

CHERRY COTTAGE PUDDING

A simple dessert for cherry lovers.

Yield: 9 servings

One 1-pound can tart red cherries in
    syrup
6 tablespoons butter or margarine
½ cup sugar
1 egg

2½ teaspoons baking powder
½ teaspoon salt
1¾ cups all-purpose flour
⅔ cup milk
1 teaspoon almond extract, optional

Sauce

One 1-pound can tart red cherries in
    syrup
1 cup (approximately) port wine
¼ cup cornstarch

¼ cup sugar
Pinch salt
2 tablespoons butter

Preheat oven to 350°F. Drain cherries and reserve syrup. Cream shortening with sugar in a mixing bowl until light and fluffy. Add egg, extract, baking powder, and salt, mixing well. Alternately add flour and milk. When mixture is well blended, gently fold in cherries and turn into a greased 8 × 8-inch baking dish. Bake at 350°F for about 30 minutes, or until toothpick inserted in middle comes out clean.

SAUCE. Drain cherries. Combine liquid with reserved liquid from first can of cherries. Measure liquid and add enough port wine to make 2½ cups. In a saucepan, combine cornstarch, sugar, and salt. Add cherry juice and wine. Cook and stir until thickened and clear. Add a few drops of red food coloring if you wish. Remove from heat, add butter, and continue stirring until butter is melted. Fold in drained cherries. Serve warm over pudding. You may wish to add vanilla ice cream or whipping cream.

PIES

GRAHAM CRACKER CRUST

Now that you can buy prepared graham cracker crumbs, this is the quickest of all the crumb crusts. It is also perhaps the best known and the most versatile.

SINGLE RECIPE	DOUBLE RECIPE
Yield: One 9-inch pie crust	*Yield: Two 9-inch pie crusts*
½ cup melted butter or margarine	1 cup melted butter or margarine
1½ cups graham cracker crumbs (or 18 crackers crushed)	3 cups graham cracker crumbs (or 36 crackers crushed)
2 tablespoons sugar	¼ cup sugar

Melt shortening. Meanwhile, measure and pour crumbs into pie plate. Add sugar and mix well. Then pour melted shortening over this mixture. Stir with a fork until all the shortening is equally incorporated in the crumb mixture. Spread mixture around evenly and press an 8-inch pie plate on top of the crumb mixture. The crumbs will shape themselves evenly. Bake at 375°F for about 8 minutes, or until edges are slightly browned. A single recipe can be mixed right in the pie tin.

VANILLA WAFER CRUST

This crust is quite a bit more crunchy than the graham cracker crust and has an entirely different flavor. Cream fillings, particularly banana cream pies, are delicious in this crust.

SINGLE RECIPE	DOUBLE RECIPE
Yield: One 9-inch crust	*Yield: Two 9-inch crusts*
1¼ cups fine vanilla wafer crumbs (about 36 cookies)	2½ cups fine vanilla wafer crumbs (about 72 cookies)
⅓ cup melted butter or margarine	⅔ cup melted butter or margarine
2 tablespoons sugar	¼ cup sugar

Wafers can be crushed quickly and easily in your blender or food processor. Melt shortening. Combine all the ingredients in the pie plate and mix thoroughly. Again, press an 8-inch pie plate on top of the crumbs to shape crust. (See instructions for Graham Cracker Crust.) Bake at 375°F for 8 minutes.

CHOCOLATE WAFER CRUST

This chocolate crust is good with any filling that goes well with chocolate. I happen to like lemon meringue filling in it, or Black Bottom Pie filling (see page 163), as well as many others.

SINGLE RECIPE
Yield: One 9-inch crust

15 (1½ cups crumbs) chocolate cream wafer cookies (two wafers held together with either vanilla or chocolate cream filling)
3 tablespoons melted butter or margarine

DOUBLE RECIPE
Yield: Two 9-inch crust

30 (3 cups crumbs) chocolate cream wafer cookies (two wafers held together with either vanilla or chocolate cream filling)
6 tablespoons melted butter or margarine

Drop cookies into the blender or food processor through the feed tube while it's going at high speed. Your crumbs will be ready in minutes. Combine with melted shortening and press into pie plate. Bake at 350°F for about 8 minutes.

CHOCOLATE COCONUT CRUST

This is an easy no-bake chocolate and coconut pie crust that's delicious.

Yield: One 9-inch pie shell

Two 1-ounce squares unsweetened chocolate
2 tablespoons butter or margarine

¾ cup unsifted powdered sugar
2 tablespoons hot water
1½ cups flaked coconut

Melt chocolate and butter over low heat. Mix powdered sugar and hot water and add chocolate mixture. Blend together until smooth. Stir in coconut. Press in bottom and sides of a buttered 9-inch pie pan. Chill.

SUGGESTED PIE FILLINGS. Coffee Soufflé (see page 155), Vanilla Bavarian Cream (see page 153), or coconut cream filling from a pudding mix.

FRUITED ONE-STEP PIE

This easy-on-the-cook pie will perk up any meal. It can be made with a number of variations from your kitchen shelf and no crust is needed. We love its chewy texture.

Yield: One 9-inch pie

One 1-pound can fruit cocktail	½ teaspoon salt
1 cup flour	1 egg
1 cup sugar	¼ cup brown sugar, packed
1½ teaspoons soda	½ cup chopped nuts

Preheat oven to 325°F. Drain fruit cocktail. Mix flour, sugar, soda, and salt. Add egg and fruit and mix gently. Mixture will become just moist. Pour into a well-greased 9-inch pie tin. Sprinkle top with brown sugar and nuts. Bake at 325°F for 30 to 40 minutes. Delicious served warm with ice cream or whipped topping.

VARIATION. Canned peaches or apricots may be substituted for fruit cocktail. Cut fruit into bite-size pieces as in fruit cocktail. Calorie-counters will be happy to know that they can use artificially sweetened canned fruit in this recipe.

OATMEAL PIE

A nutritious sweet for your sweet tooth. Can be made with or without a crust.

Yield: One 9-inch pie

3 eggs, well beaten	1 teaspoon vanilla
¾ cup brown sugar, packed	½ teaspoon baking powder
1 cup quick-cooking rolled oats	½ cup buttermilk
1 cup coconut flakes	½ cup currants
2 tablespoons melted margarine	1 unbaked 9-inch pie shell

Preheat oven to 375°F. Beat eggs with brown sugar until well blended. Add rolled oats, coconut, melted margarine, vanilla, baking powder, buttermilk, and currants. Blend until all the ingredients are thoroughly combined. Turn into unbaked pie shell and bake at 375°F for 25 to 30 minutes, or until set. If you wish to eliminate the pie crust, just pour into a generously buttered pie pan.

BLACK BOTTOM PIE

This pie is particularly good made with Chocolate Wafer Crust (see page 162). A fantastic flavor combination.

Yield: One 9-inch pie

1 envelope unflavored gelatin
⅓ cup rum
1 cup milk
4 egg yolks

½ cup chocolate chips
One Chocolate Wafer Crust
½ pint whipping cream, whipped
Chocolate curls (optional)

Dissolve gelatin in rum. This can be done in your blender or food processor. Place rum in blender and add gelatin; let it dissolve for 3 minutes.

Meanwhile, bring milk to scalding point. Add to softened gelatin and twirl at medium speed until gelatin is dissolved. At low speed, add egg yolks one at a time, blending mixture until thick. Remove one cup of gelatin mixture and combine with chocolate chips. Continue stirring until all the chocolate is dissolved. Pour into prepared crust. Whip cream; fold remaining gelatin mixture into whipped cream. Pour on top of the chocolate mixture, mounding as you go. Garnish with chocolate curls. Refrigerate several hours before serving.

IMPOSSIBLE COCONUT PIE

I'm not sure if this dessert was named because it is impossible to have a failure, or because the recipe seems unlikely to turn into a pie. Either way, it's a fun and easy recipe with good taste appeal and several variations.

Yield: One 10-inch pie

4 eggs
¾ cup sugar
2 cups milk
1 teaspoon vanilla
½ cup biscuit mix

¼ cup butter or margarine
One 7-ounce package flaked coconut
2 ounces unsweetened chocolate,
    melted (optional)

Preheat oven to 350°F. In blender, combine eggs with sugar. Add milk, vanilla, biscuit mix and butter or margarine, mixing until all the ingredients are well blended. Sprinkle coconut in bottom of generously greased pie dish. Pour blended mixture over coconut. Bake at 350°F for 40 minutes or until golden brown and crust has formed.

VARIATIONS. For Chocolate Coconut Pie, melt 2 ounces of unsweetened chocolate with butter and add ¼ cup more sugar to egg mixture. The chocolate doesn't blend smoothly, but don't worry about it. As the pie bakes, a white crust forms, with a chocolate filling!

Pineapple Coconut Pie can be made by adding a well-drained 20-ounce can of crushed pineapple to coconut in bottom of pie dish. To reserved pineapple juice, add enough milk to measure 1¾ cups. Then proceed as above.

CAKES, COBBLERS, AND CRISPS

BLUEBERRY CAKE

This is a melt-in-your-mouth old-fashioned type blueberry "coffee cake." It can be made in advance, as it keeps well in the refrigerator and in the freezer.

Yield: One 9 × 13-inch pan cake

¼ pound (½ cup) butter or margarine
1 cup sugar
3 eggs
2 teaspoons baking powder
½ teaspoon salt
1 teaspoon vanilla

2 cups sifted flour
1 pint fresh blueberries, or 2 cups frozen blueberries, drained and thawed
2–3 tablespoons sugar
½ teaspoon cinnamon

Preheat oven to 350°F. Cream butter and sugar until light and fluffy. Add eggs one at a time, beating well after each addition. Add baking powder, salt, and vanilla, again mixing well. Add flour, Now fold in blueberries. Spread in a well greased 9 × 13-inch baking dish. Combine cinnamon and sugar. Sprinkle lightly over the top. Bake in a 350°F oven for approximately 45 minutes, or until cake feels done when you test it.

FUDGE CAKE

This moist chocolate cake can be baked as a pan cake or as a layer cake.

Yield: One 9 × 13-inch pan cake, or three 8-inch layers

¾ cup butter or margarine
2¼ cups sugar
1½ teaspoons vanilla
3 eggs
1½ teaspoons baking soda

¾ teaspoons salt
Three 1-ounce squares unsweetened chocolate, melted
2½ cups sifted all-purpose flour
1½ cups ice water

Preheat oven to 350°F. Cream butter, sugar, and vanilla together until light and fluffy. Add eggs and beat well. Add baking soda, salt, and melted chocolate; blend well. Alternately add flour and ice water. Pour batter into three 8-inch round layer cake pans that have been greased and lined with waxed paper, or one greased 9 × 13-inch baking dish. Bake at 350°F for about 30 minutes. Cool and frost with Fudge Frosting (see page 166).

Fudge Frosting

A quick and easy dark chocolate frosting.

*Yield: Sufficient to frost sides
and top of an 8-inch 3-layer
cake, or top of one
9 × 13-inch pan cake*

2 tablespoons butter or margarine
Three 1-ounce squares unsweetened
  chocolate
2 cups sifted confectioners sugar

6 tablespoons light cream or
  evaporated milk
Pinch salt
1 teaspoon vanilla

Melt butter and chocolate in a saucepan over hot water or very low heat (or in your microwave oven). Add 1½ cups of the sifted confectioners sugar, cream, and salt, all at one time. Beat until smooth. Continue cooking over low heat, stirring constantly, until bubbles appear on the edge of the pan. Add vanilla and remaining confectioners sugar a small amount at a time, beating well after each addition. Cool in ice water until thick enough to spread easily.

Dark Chocolate Glaze

A not-too-sweet quick recipe.

*Yield: Sufficient frosting to
cover a 9 × 13-inch pan cake*

Two 1-ounce squares unsweetened
  chocolate
1 tablespoon butter or margarine

1 cup confectioners sugar, sifted
2 tablespoons water

Over very low heat or boiling water, or in microwave oven, melt chocolate with butter. Stir in confectioners sugar alternately with water until mixture is well blended and smooth.

VARIATION. Chocolate sauce can be made from this glaze by adding 1 or 2 tablespoons of water. It's good served over sundaes and banana splits, eclairs, and cream puffs.

1-2-3 CREAMY CHEESE CAKE (NO-BAKE)

This marvelous cheese cake can be put together, from start to finish, in less than 10 minutes. There are many variations to this basic recipe, all of them delicious.

Yield: One 9-inch cheese cake

1 cup corn flake crumbs
⅓ cup butter or margarine, melted
1 package (1 tablespoon) unflavored
  gelatin
¼ cup water, brandy, or rum

Three 8-ounce packages cream
  cheese
1 cup sifted confectioners sugar
½ pint (1 cup) whipping cream

Preheat oven to 375°F. Place corn flake crumbs in the bottom of a 9-inch spring form pan. Pour melted butter or margarine over the crumbs and pat evenly over bottom. You may wish to bake this crust for about 5 minutes to make it less crumbly. However, this is not necessary.

In a small Pyrex container or measuring cup dissolve gelatin in water or liquor for 3 minutes. Heat over low heat or in your microwave oven until gelatin is dissolved. Cream the cream cheese until light and fluffy. Sift in sugar and continue mixing until blended. Add dissolved gelatin, mixing well.

In a separate bowl, whip cream until quite stiff. Fold into cream cheese mixture. Pour mixture into prepared spring form pan. Refrigerate about 1 to 2 hours before serving.

ORANGE OR LEMON CHEESE CAKE. Frozen orange juice or lemonade concentrate, thawed, can be substituted for the water or brandy and used to dissolve the gelatin. Add an additional ¼ cup frozen concentrate to the cream cheese mixture, making a total of ½ cup.

STRAWBERRY CHEESE CAKE. Thaw one 10- or 16-ounce package of frozen strawberries. Use ¼ cup of the juice to dissolve the gelatin. Put remaining strawberries and juice in blender and blend until smooth. Add to cream cheese mixture along with gelatin.

CREAMY CHOCOLATE CHEESE CAKE. Dissolve gelatin in ¼ cup crème de cacao or water, whichever you prefer. Add 1 teaspoon of vanilla to cream cheese mixture, along with ¼ cup crème de cacao (optional). Over very low heat, melt 6 ounces of semisweet chocolate. Fold into cream cheese mixture before adding the whipped cream.

ST. PATRICK'S DAY SPECIAL. Add some green food coloring and some Irish whiskey in place of the brandy to dissolve the gelatin. Crème de menthe would be another good flavor to use.

OTHER VARIATIONS. Make a vanilla cheese cake by adding 1 teaspoon vanilla to the cream cheese mixture, and top it with a can of cherry or blueberry pie filling. As you can see, the variations are infinite.

GOURMANDS

There's no point in throwing out stale cakes and cookies when you can turn them into this delectable dessert. Grate, blend, or process any leftover or stale cakes or cookies into crumbs and save in refrigerator or freezer until you have enough for this recipe. This is a good recipe to remember when you overbake a cake and it's very dry, or just bake a "flop."

Yield: Approximately 24
  1½-inch balls

4 cups stale cake or cookie crumbs
One 14-ounce carton raspberry filling
½ cup ground or finely chopped
  almonds (optional)

2 ounces grated sweet chocolate
  (optional)
½ to ¾ cup rum
Shredded coconut, plain or toasted

Combine cake crumbs with raspberry filling (available in the baking products section at your supermarket). Add almonds or grated chocolate or both if desired. Now add enough rum to moisten. When mixture is slightly gooky, set in refrigerator to chill for 1 hour. Remove from refrigerator and form into 1½-inch balls. Roll in coconut and set on a cookie tray that has been lined with waxed paper or bakery paper. Refrigerate until ready to serve. (If this is going to be an extended period of time, you'll want to cover them before refrigerating.)

TO FREEZE. These balls may be frozen in an airtight container. The Tupperware pie-taker is flat and the perfect size for storing these. When you're ready to serve them, simply remove from freezer and thaw to room temperature.

VARIATION. Brandy, a fruited liqueur, or dry red wine may be substituted for the rum.

VERMONT APPLE COBBLER

Really an old-fashioned dessert. Quick to make if you use frozen apple slices.

Yield: 6 servings

6 medium size apples, peeled, cored,
  and sliced, or approximately 5
  cups apple slices
½ cup maple syrup
¼ cup butter or margarine
½ cup sugar

1 egg
2 teaspoons baking powder
½ teaspoon salt
1 cup flour
¼ cup milk

Preheat oven to 400°F. Put the apples in the bottom of a greased 8 × 8-inch baking dish. Cover with maple syrup and toss until all the apples are coated.

In a mixing bowl cream butter with sugar until creamy. Add egg, baking powder, and salt. Alternately add flour and milk, blending until mixture is smooth. Spoon over apple slices, spreading evenly with a rubber spatula. Bake at 400°F for 25 to 30 minutes, or until topping is golden brown and apples feel done when tested. Serve warm with plain cream, whipped cream, or ice cream.

PEACH CRISP

A quick and delicious recipe to make with fresh or frozen peaches.

Yield: 6 to 8 servings

7 to 8 large peaches, peeled and sliced (about six cups)
3 tablespoons lemon juice
1 cup flour

¾ cup brown sugar, packed
1 teaspoon cinnamon
¼ teaspoon nutmeg
½ cup butter or margarine

Preheat oven to 375°F. Drop fresh peaches in a pan of boiling water for a few seconds and the peelings will just slip off. Slice peaches into a buttered 8 × 8-inch glass baking dish. Sprinkle with lemon juice and toss. In a separate bowl or in your food processor, combine flour, brown sugar, and spices. Cut in butter with a pastry blender, food processor, or mixer until mixture is crumbly (when you use your food processor be careful not to overprocess). Spread over the top of the peaches and bake at 375°F for 30 minutes, or until peaches are tender and mixture is well browned and bubbly. Remove from oven and serve warm with cream or vanilla ice cream.

OLD-FASHIONED BLUEBERRY BUCKLE

Truly a mouth-watering dessert.

Yield: One 8 × 8-inch cake,
*   which serves not nearly as*
*   many as you thought it would*

½ cup shortening
¾ cup sugar
2 eggs, separated
2 teaspoons baking powder

½ teaspoon salt
½ cup milk
1½ cups sifted flour
1 pint blueberries

Topping

⅓ cup sugar
½ cup sifted flour

½ teaspoon cinnamon
¼ cup butter

Preheat oven to 350°F. Cream shortening and sugar; add egg yolks one at a time and beat well. Add baking powder and salt. When mixture is well blended, alternately add milk and flour, beating well after each addition. Fold in stiffly beaten egg whites and pour into greased 8 × 8 × 2-inch baking pan. Top with washed and well drained blueberries. Sprinkle with topping and bake in a 350°F oven for 30 minutes. Serve warm.

TOPPING. Combine sugar, flour, and cinnamon. Cut in butter until mixture is crumbly. Sprinkle on top of cake.

VARIATION. Pour half the batter in the pan, sprinkle with blueberries, and cover with remaining batter. Then add topping.

BAVARIAN PLUM FLAN

You've seen this picturesque flan in continental and European bakery shops and restaurants. It's easy to make.

Yield: One 9-inch flan

Approximately 18 Italian blue plums	Pinch salt
⅓ cup butter or margarine	¾ cup flour
⅓ cup sugar	1½ tablespoons sugar
2 eggs	½ teaspoon cinnamon
¼ teaspoon vanilla extract	½ teaspoon mace
⅛ teaspoon almond extract	

Topping

½ cup almonds, ground or blended fine	1 tablespoon brown sugar
2 tablespoons butter	1 tablespoon flour

Preheat oven to 375°F. Wash and halve plums. In a small mixing bowl cream butter and sugar until light and fluffy. Add eggs one at a time, beating well after each addition. Add extracts and salt. Blend in flour. Butter a 9-inch flan or spring form pan (with a removable bottom) and spread batter evenly over the bottom of pan. Arrange the plum halves cut side up, covering batter, and sprinkle with sugar that has been mixed with cinnamon and mace. Bake at 375°F for 20 minutes.

TOPPING. Combine almonds with butter, brown sugar, and flour. Remove cake after 20 minutes of baking and sprinkle this mixture over the top. Return to oven and bake for an additional 10 minutes or until cake feels done when tested. This dessert is best served warm.

CREAM PUFFS

These cream puffs are made with vegetable oil instead of butter. You'll be amazed how quickly they are put together and how large they are. Make them ahead of time and store them in plastic bags, tightly sealed. They'll keep for weeks! A never-fail recipe.

*Yield: 1 dozen very large cream
   puffs, or 3 dozen small cream
   puffs*

1 cup water	1 cup flour (not sifted)
½ cup vegetable oil	4 eggs
1 teaspoon salt	

Preheat oven to 450°F. In a medium size saucepan heat water to boiling. Add vegetable oil and salt. Continue cooking until mixture boils again. Remove from heat and add flour all at once, mixing until mixture pulls away from side of pan. Put in mixing bowl and beat with mixer at low speed. Add eggs one at a time, mixing well after each, and beat until mixture is shiny. Continue beating until all four eggs have been added. Mixture should be smooth, shiny, and soft. Drop by large tablespoon for large cream puffs, or rounded teaspoon for small puffs, onto ungreased baking sheet about 2 inches apart. Bake at 450°F for 15 minutes. Reduce heat to 350°F and bake for an additional 20 minutes. Turn off oven, leave door open, and cool slowly in oven.

Filling

Yield: Sufficient filling for about 8 large cream puffs

1 pint heavy cream
½ cup Kahlua

Beat cream until quite stiff. Add Kahlua one tablespoon at a time, whipping slowly. When all the liqueur has been added, chill until ready to serve.

Chocolate Sauce

Yield: 1½ cups

1 cup hot fudge sauce, purchased or homemade
½ cup Kahlua

Pour fudge sauce into a small skillet or saucepan and warm gently over low heat. Add Kahlua, stirring until mixture is well blended and warm. Remove from heat and set aside until serving time.

TO SERVE. Slice tops off cream puffs, fill with whipped cream filling, replace tops and refrigerate until serving time. Just before serving spoon Chocolate Sauce over cream puffs.

VARIATIONS. Cream puffs can be filled with any of the Blender Desserts (see page 153). Fill shortly before serving so puffs don't get soggy.

Pudding and pie mixes as well as ice creams, also make good fillings. Keep these puffs on hand for unexpected guests. Crisp in oven at 350°F for 5 minutes, if necessary.

Index

Cuisinart Food Processor Model DLC-7

Features: Only 7¾ inches wide by 10½ inches deep and 15 inches high. One year warranty (full 30-year warranty as to rotor, stator, and motor shaft bearings). Cuisinart DLC-7 has a metal blade (chopping, mixing), short plastic blade for mixing dough, serrated slicing disc, shredding disc. Bowl capacity holds almost half again as much as the bowl on earlier models. Uses up to 6 cups of flour (3 pounds of bread dough) in 90 seconds. Booklet includes 40 pages of instructions and recipes.

Sunbeam Food Preparation Center

Features: A 450-watt motor; one year warranty; three appliances in one: blender, food processor, and mixer. The food processor comes with a steel cutting plate, a shredding plate, and a slicing plate, along with a food pusher that can double as a measuring cup. The blender has a 5-quart capacity, and the mixer comes with two stainless steel bowls, a large one with a 4½-quart capacity, the small one with a 2½-quart capacity, along with a set of beaters as well as dough hooks. A 110-page instruction and recipe booklet.

Comments: The advantage of having these three appliances in one is that it takes up less space, having one unit and its attachments instead of three, as well as costing less. The food processor can work at variable speeds which is a great advantage. Slicing soft foods, such as bananas and mushrooms, at the lower speeds works infinitely better than with a constantly high speed. Machine has good safety features, and the idea of having two stainless steel bowls is very attractive for anyone who is into baking. The instruction booklet is not very inspiring. Some of it seems as though it hadn't been tested on the machine, and some of the instructions are erroneous. The mixer is rather loud at high speeds; the food processor does not have an automatic circuit breaker and does slow down when mixing heavy loads, such as kneading bread dough. The capacity of the food processor is 3½ cups of flour. It also loses stability and tends to "walk" with heavy loads in the food processor. One of the big disadvantages is that it is difficult and time consuming to switch from using the unit as a food processor to using it as a mixing unit. This can be rather frustrating if you are baking or cooking something that requires both units for efficiency. If you are chopping nuts, making cake fillings, etc., in the food processor while at the same time mixing your cake batter in the mixer, your steps would have to be well thought out in advance. This would not be a problem for someone who just mixes up an occasional cake and only does a moderate amount of cooking.